C-4464　　**CAREER EXAMINATION SERIES**

This is your
PASSBOOK for...

Rehabilitation Counselor II

Test Preparation Study Guide
Questions & Answers

COPYRIGHT NOTICE

This book is SOLELY intended for, is sold ONLY to, and its use is RESTRICTED to individual, bona fide applicants or candidates who qualify by virtue of having seriously filed applications for appropriate license, certificate, professional and/or promotional advancement, higher school matriculation, scholarship, or other legitimate requirements of education and/or governmental authorities.

This book is NOT intended for use, class instruction, tutoring, training, duplication, copying, reprinting, excerption, or adaptation, etc., by:

1) Other publishers
2) Proprietors and/or Instructors of "Coaching" and/or Preparatory Courses
3) Personnel and/or Training Divisions of commercial, industrial, and governmental organizations
4) Schools, colleges, or universities and/or their departments and staffs, including teachers and other personnel
5) Testing Agencies or Bureaus
6) Study groups which seek by the purchase of a single volume to copy and/or duplicate and/or adapt this material for use by the group as a whole without having purchased individual volumes for each of the members of the group
7) Et al.

Such persons would be in violation of appropriate Federal and State statutes.

PROVISION OF LICENSING AGREEMENTS – Recognized educational, commercial, industrial, and governmental institutions and organizations, and others legitimately engaged in educational pursuits, including training, testing, and measurement activities, may address request for a licensing agreement to the copyright owners, who will determine whether, and under what conditions, including fees and charges, the materials in this book may be used them. In other words, a licensing facility exists for the legitimate use of the material in this book on other than an individual basis. However, it is asseverated and affirmed here that the material in this book CANNOT be used without the receipt of the express permission of such a licensing agreement from the Publishers. Inquiries re licensing should be addressed to the company, attention rights and permissions department.

All rights reserved, including the right of reproduction in whole or in part, in any form or by any means, electronic or mechanical, including photocopying, recording, or by any information storage and retrieval system, without permission in writing from the Publisher.

Copyright © 2024 by
National Learning Corporation

212 Michael Drive, Syosset, NY 11791
(516) 921-8888 • www.passbooks.com
E-mail: info@passbooks.com

PASSBOOK® SERIES

THE *PASSBOOK® SERIES* has been created to prepare applicants and candidates for the ultimate academic battlefield – the examination room.

At some time in our lives, each and every one of us may be required to take an examination – for validation, matriculation, admission, qualification, registration, certification, or licensure.

Based on the assumption that every applicant or candidate has met the basic formal educational standards, has taken the required number of courses, and read the necessary texts, the *PASSBOOK® SERIES* furnishes the one special preparation which may assure passing with confidence, instead of failing with insecurity. Examination questions – together with answers – are furnished as the basic vehicle for study so that the mysteries of the examination and its compounding difficulties may be eliminated or diminished by a sure method.

This book is meant to help you pass your examination provided that you qualify and are serious in your objective.

The entire field is reviewed through the huge store of content information which is succinctly presented through a provocative and challenging approach – the question-and-answer method.

A climate of success is established by furnishing the correct answers at the end of each test.

You soon learn to recognize types of questions, forms of questions, and patterns of questioning. You may even begin to anticipate expected outcomes.

You perceive that many questions are repeated or adapted so that you can gain acute insights, which may enable you to score many sure points.

You learn how to confront new questions, or types of questions, and to attack them confidently and work out the correct answers.

You note objectives and emphases, and recognize pitfalls and dangers, so that you may make positive educational adjustments.

Moreover, you are kept fully informed in relation to new concepts, methods, practices, and directions in the field.

You discover that you are actually taking the examination all the time: you are preparing for the examination by "taking" an examination, not by reading extraneous and/or supererogatory textbooks.

In short, this PASSBOOK®, used directedly, should be an important factor in helping you to pass your test.

REHABILITATION COUNSELOR II

DUTIES
Performs specialized services in the vocational rehabilitation of correctional institution inmates, hospital patients with physical or mental illness, or substance abusers; performs related duties as requires.

SUBJECT OF EXAMINATION
Written test will cover knowledge, skills, and/or abilities in such areas as:
1. Acquiring and maintaining employment;
2. Principles and practices of employment counseling;
3. Case histories of employment clients;
4. Interviewing; and
5. Preparing written material.

HOW TO TAKE A TEST

I. YOU MUST PASS AN EXAMINATION

A. WHAT EVERY CANDIDATE SHOULD KNOW

Examination applicants often ask us for help in preparing for the written test. What can I study in advance? What kinds of questions will be asked? How will the test be given? How will the papers be graded?

As an applicant for a civil service examination, you may be wondering about some of these things. Our purpose here is to suggest effective methods of advance study and to describe civil service examinations.

Your chances for success on this examination can be increased if you know how to prepare. Those "pre-examination jitters" can be reduced if you know what to expect. You can even experience an adventure in good citizenship if you know why civil service exams are given.

B. WHY ARE CIVIL SERVICE EXAMINATIONS GIVEN?

Civil service examinations are important to you in two ways. As a citizen, you want public jobs filled by employees who know how to do their work. As a job seeker, you want a fair chance to compete for that job on an equal footing with other candidates. The best-known means of accomplishing this two-fold goal is the competitive examination.

Exams are widely publicized throughout the nation. They may be administered for jobs in federal, state, city, municipal, town or village governments or agencies.

Any citizen may apply, with some limitations, such as the age or residence of applicants. Your experience and education may be reviewed to see whether you meet the requirements for the particular examination. When these requirements exist, they are reasonable and applied consistently to all applicants. Thus, a competitive examination may cause you some uneasiness now, but it is your privilege and safeguard.

C. HOW ARE CIVIL SERVICE EXAMS DEVELOPED?

Examinations are carefully written by trained technicians who are specialists in the field known as "psychological measurement," in consultation with recognized authorities in the field of work that the test will cover. These experts recommend the subject matter areas or skills to be tested; only those knowledges or skills important to your success on the job are included. The most reliable books and source materials available are used as references. Together, the experts and technicians judge the difficulty level of the questions.

Test technicians know how to phrase questions so that the problem is clearly stated. Their ethics do not permit "trick" or "catch" questions. Questions may have been tried out on sample groups, or subjected to statistical analysis, to determine their usefulness.

Written tests are often used in combination with performance tests, ratings of training and experience, and oral interviews. All of these measures combine to form the best-known means of finding the right person for the right job.

II. HOW TO PASS THE WRITTEN TEST

A. NATURE OF THE EXAMINATION

To prepare intelligently for civil service examinations, you should know how they differ from school examinations you have taken. In school you were assigned certain definite pages to read or subjects to cover. The examination questions were quite detailed and usually emphasized memory. Civil service exams, on the other hand, try to discover your present ability to perform the duties of a position, plus your potentiality to learn these duties. In other words, a civil service exam attempts to predict how successful you will be. Questions cover such a broad area that they cannot be as minute and detailed as school exam questions.

In the public service similar kinds of work, or positions, are grouped together in one "class." This process is known as *position-classification*. All the positions in a class are paid according to the salary range for that class. One class title covers all of these positions, and they are all tested by the same examination.

B. FOUR BASIC STEPS

1) Study the announcement

How, then, can you know what subjects to study? Our best answer is: "Learn as much as possible about the class of positions for which you've applied." The exam will test the knowledge, skills and abilities needed to do the work.

Your most valuable source of information about the position you want is the official exam announcement. This announcement lists the training and experience qualifications. Check these standards and apply only if you come reasonably close to meeting them.

The brief description of the position in the examination announcement offers some clues to the subjects which will be tested. Think about the job itself. Review the duties in your mind. Can you perform them, or are there some in which you are rusty? Fill in the blank spots in your preparation.

Many jurisdictions preview the written test in the exam announcement by including a section called "Knowledge and Abilities Required," "Scope of the Examination," or some similar heading. Here you will find out specifically what fields will be tested.

2) Review your own background

Once you learn in general what the position is all about, and what you need to know to do the work, ask yourself which subjects you already know fairly well and which need improvement. You may wonder whether to concentrate on improving your strong areas or on building some background in your fields of weakness. When the announcement has specified "some knowledge" or "considerable knowledge," or has used adjectives like "beginning principles of..." or "advanced ... methods," you can get a clue as to the number and difficulty of questions to be asked in any given field. More questions, and hence broader coverage, would be included for those subjects which are more important in the work. Now weigh your strengths and weaknesses against the job requirements and prepare accordingly.

3) Determine the level of the position

Another way to tell how intensively you should prepare is to understand the level of the job for which you are applying. Is it the entering level? In other words, is this the position in which beginners in a field of work are hired? Or is it an intermediate or advanced level? Sometimes this is indicated by such words as "Junior" or "Senior" in the class title. Other jurisdictions use Roman numerals to designate the level – Clerk I, Clerk II, for example. The word "Supervisor" sometimes appears in the title. If the level is not indicated by the title, check the description of duties. Will you be working under very close supervision, or will you have responsibility for independent decisions in this work?

4) Choose appropriate study materials

Now that you know the subjects to be examined and the relative amount of each subject to be covered, you can choose suitable study materials. For beginning level jobs, or even advanced ones, if you have a pronounced weakness in some aspect of your training, read a modern, standard textbook in that field. Be sure it is up to date and has general coverage. Such books are normally available at your library, and the librarian will be glad to help you locate one. For entry-level positions, questions of appropriate difficulty are chosen -- neither highly advanced questions, nor those too simple. Such questions require careful thought but not advanced training.

If the position for which you are applying is technical or advanced, you will read more advanced, specialized material. If you are already familiar with the basic principles of your field, elementary textbooks would waste your time. Concentrate on advanced textbooks and technical periodicals. Think through the concepts and review difficult problems in your field.

These are all general sources. You can get more ideas on your own initiative, following these leads. For example, training manuals and publications of the government agency which employs workers in your field can be useful, particularly for technical and professional positions. A letter or visit to the government department involved may result in more specific study suggestions, and certainly will provide you with a more definite idea of the exact nature of the position you are seeking.

III. KINDS OF TESTS

Tests are used for purposes other than measuring knowledge and ability to perform specified duties. For some positions, it is equally important to test ability to make adjustments to new situations or to profit from training. In others, basic mental abilities not dependent on information are essential. Questions which test these things may not appear as pertinent to the duties of the position as those which test for knowledge and information. Yet they are often highly important parts of a fair examination. For very general questions, it is almost impossible to help you direct your study efforts. What we can do is to point out some of the more common of these general abilities needed in public service positions and describe some typical questions.

1) General information

Broad, general information has been found useful for predicting job success in some kinds of work. This is tested in a variety of ways, from vocabulary lists to questions about current events. Basic background in some field of work, such as sociology or economics, may be sampled in a group of questions. Often these are principles which have become familiar to most persons through exposure rather than through formal training. It is difficult to advise you how to study for these questions; being alert to the world around you is our best suggestion.

2) Verbal ability

An example of an ability needed in many positions is verbal or language ability. Verbal ability is, in brief, the ability to use and understand words. Vocabulary and grammar tests are typical measures of this ability. Reading comprehension or paragraph interpretation questions are common in many kinds of civil service tests. You are given a paragraph of written material and asked to find its central meaning.

3) Numerical ability

Number skills can be tested by the familiar arithmetic problem, by checking paired lists of numbers to see which are alike and which are different, or by interpreting charts and graphs. In the latter test, a graph may be printed in the test booklet which you are asked to use as the basis for answering questions.

4) Observation

A popular test for law-enforcement positions is the observation test. A picture is shown to you for several minutes, then taken away. Questions about the picture test your ability to observe both details and larger elements.

5) Following directions

In many positions in the public service, the employee must be able to carry out written instructions dependably and accurately. You may be given a chart with several columns, each column listing a variety of information. The questions require you to carry out directions involving the information given in the chart.

6) Skills and aptitudes

Performance tests effectively measure some manual skills and aptitudes. When the skill is one in which you are trained, such as typing or shorthand, you can practice. These tests are often very much like those given in business school or high school courses. For many of the other skills and aptitudes, however, no short-time preparation can be made. Skills and abilities natural to you or that you have developed throughout your lifetime are being tested.

Many of the general questions just described provide all the data needed to answer the questions and ask you to use your reasoning ability to find the answers. Your best preparation for these tests, as well as for tests of facts and ideas, is to be at your physical and mental best. You, no doubt, have your own methods of getting into an exam-taking mood and keeping "in shape." The next section lists some ideas on this subject.

IV. KINDS OF QUESTIONS

Only rarely is the "essay" question, which you answer in narrative form, used in civil service tests. Civil service tests are usually of the short-answer type. Full instructions for answering these questions will be given to you at the examination. But in case this is your first experience with short-answer questions and separate answer sheets, here is what you need to know:

1) Multiple-choice Questions

Most popular of the short-answer questions is the "multiple choice" or "best answer" question. It can be used, for example, to test for factual knowledge, ability to solve problems or judgment in meeting situations found at work.

A multiple-choice question is normally one of three types—
- It can begin with an incomplete statement followed by several possible endings. You are to find the one ending which *best* completes the statement, although some of the others may not be entirely wrong.
- It can also be a complete statement in the form of a question which is answered by choosing one of the statements listed.

- It can be in the form of a problem – again you select the best answer.

Here is an example of a multiple-choice question with a discussion which should give you some clues as to the method for choosing the right answer:

When an employee has a complaint about his assignment, the action which will *best* help him overcome his difficulty is to
- A. discuss his difficulty with his coworkers
- B. take the problem to the head of the organization
- C. take the problem to the person who gave him the assignment
- D. say nothing to anyone about his complaint

In answering this question, you should study each of the choices to find which is best. Consider choice "A" – Certainly an employee may discuss his complaint with fellow employees, but no change or improvement can result, and the complaint remains unresolved. Choice "B" is a poor choice since the head of the organization probably does not know what assignment you have been given, and taking your problem to him is known as "going over the head" of the supervisor. The supervisor, or person who made the assignment, is the person who can clarify it or correct any injustice. Choice "C" is, therefore, correct. To say nothing, as in choice "D," is unwise. Supervisors have and interest in knowing the problems employees are facing, and the employee is seeking a solution to his problem.

2) True/False Questions

The "true/false" or "right/wrong" form of question is sometimes used. Here a complete statement is given. Your job is to decide whether the statement is right or wrong.

SAMPLE: A roaming cell-phone call to a nearby city costs less than a non-roaming call to a distant city.

This statement is wrong, or false, since roaming calls are more expensive.

This is not a complete list of all possible question forms, although most of the others are variations of these common types. You will always get complete directions for answering questions. Be sure you understand *how* to mark your answers – ask questions until you do.

V. RECORDING YOUR ANSWERS

Computer terminals are used more and more today for many different kinds of exams.

For an examination with very few applicants, you may be told to record your answers in the test booklet itself. Separate answer sheets are much more common. If this separate answer sheet is to be scored by machine – and this is often the case – it is highly important that you mark your answers correctly in order to get credit.

An electronic scoring machine is often used in civil service offices because of the speed with which papers can be scored. Machine-scored answer sheets must be marked with a pencil, which will be given to you. This pencil has a high graphite content which responds to the electronic scoring machine. As a matter of fact, stray dots may register as answers, so do not let your pencil rest on the answer sheet while you are pondering the correct answer. Also, if your pencil lead breaks or is otherwise defective, ask for another.

Since the answer sheet will be dropped in a slot in the scoring machine, be careful not to bend the corners or get the paper crumpled.

The answer sheet normally has five vertical columns of numbers, with 30 numbers to a column. These numbers correspond to the question numbers in your test booklet. After each number, going across the page are four or five pairs of dotted lines. These short dotted lines have small letters or numbers above them. The first two pairs may also have a "T" or "F" above the letters. This indicates that the first two pairs only are to be used if the questions are of the true-false type. If the questions are multiple choice, disregard the "T" and "F" and pay attention only to the small letters or numbers.

Answer your questions in the manner of the sample that follows:

32. The largest city in the United States is
    A. Washington, D.C.
    B. New York City
    C. Chicago
    D. Detroit
    E. San Francisco

1) Choose the answer you think is best. (New York City is the largest, so "B" is correct.)
2) Find the row of dotted lines numbered the same as the question you are answering. (Find row number 32)
3) Find the pair of dotted lines corresponding to the answer. (Find the pair of lines under the mark "B.")
4) Make a solid black mark between the dotted lines.

VI. BEFORE THE TEST

Common sense will help you find procedures to follow to get ready for an examination. Too many of us, however, overlook these sensible measures. Indeed, nervousness and fatigue have been found to be the most serious reasons why applicants fail to do their best on civil service tests. Here is a list of reminders:

- Begin your preparation early – Don't wait until the last minute to go scurrying around for books and materials or to find out what the position is all about.
- Prepare continuously – An hour a night for a week is better than an all-night cram session. This has been definitely established. What is more, a night a week for a month will return better dividends than crowding your study into a shorter period of time.
- Locate the place of the exam – You have been sent a notice telling you when and where to report for the examination. If the location is in a different town or otherwise unfamiliar to you, it would be well to inquire the best route and learn something about the building.
- Relax the night before the test – Allow your mind to rest. Do not study at all that night. Plan some mild recreation or diversion; then go to bed early and get a good night's sleep.
- Get up early enough to make a leisurely trip to the place for the test – This way unforeseen events, traffic snarls, unfamiliar buildings, etc. will not upset you.
- Dress comfortably – A written test is not a fashion show. You will be known by number and not by name, so wear something comfortable.

- Leave excess paraphernalia at home – Shopping bags and odd bundles will get in your way. You need bring only the items mentioned in the official notice you received; usually everything you need is provided. Do not bring reference books to the exam. They will only confuse those last minutes and be taken away from you when in the test room.
- Arrive somewhat ahead of time – If because of transportation schedules you must get there very early, bring a newspaper or magazine to take your mind off yourself while waiting.
- Locate the examination room – When you have found the proper room, you will be directed to the seat or part of the room where you will sit. Sometimes you are given a sheet of instructions to read while you are waiting. Do not fill out any forms until you are told to do so; just read them and be prepared.
- Relax and prepare to listen to the instructions
- If you have any physical problem that may keep you from doing your best, be sure to tell the test administrator. If you are sick or in poor health, you really cannot do your best on the exam. You can come back and take the test some other time.

VII. AT THE TEST

The day of the test is here and you have the test booklet in your hand. The temptation to get going is very strong. Caution! There is more to success than knowing the right answers. You must know how to identify your papers and understand variations in the type of short-answer question used in this particular examination. Follow these suggestions for maximum results from your efforts:

1) Cooperate with the monitor

The test administrator has a duty to create a situation in which you can be as much at ease as possible. He will give instructions, tell you when to begin, check to see that you are marking your answer sheet correctly, and so on. He is not there to guard you, although he will see that your competitors do not take unfair advantage. He wants to help you do your best.

2) Listen to all instructions

Don't jump the gun! Wait until you understand all directions. In most civil service tests you get more time than you need to answer the questions. So don't be in a hurry. Read each word of instructions until you clearly understand the meaning. Study the examples, listen to all announcements and follow directions. Ask questions if you do not understand what to do.

3) Identify your papers

Civil service exams are usually identified by number only. You will be assigned a number; you must not put your name on your test papers. Be sure to copy your number correctly. Since more than one exam may be given, copy your exact examination title.

4) Plan your time

Unless you are told that a test is a "speed" or "rate of work" test, speed itself is usually not important. Time enough to answer all the questions will be provided, but this does not mean that you have all day. An overall time limit has been set. Divide the total time (in minutes) by the number of questions to determine the approximate time you have for each question.

5) Do not linger over difficult questions

If you come across a difficult question, mark it with a paper clip (useful to have along) and come back to it when you have been through the booklet. One caution if you do this – be sure to skip a number on your answer sheet as well. Check often to be sure that you have not lost your place and that you are marking in the row numbered the same as the question you are answering.

6) Read the questions

Be sure you know what the question asks! Many capable people are unsuccessful because they failed to *read* the questions correctly.

7) Answer all questions

Unless you have been instructed that a penalty will be deducted for incorrect answers, it is better to guess than to omit a question.

8) Speed tests

It is often better NOT to guess on speed tests. It has been found that on timed tests people are tempted to spend the last few seconds before time is called in marking answers at random – without even reading them – in the hope of picking up a few extra points. To discourage this practice, the instructions may warn you that your score will be "corrected" for guessing. That is, a penalty will be applied. The incorrect answers will be deducted from the correct ones, or some other penalty formula will be used.

9) Review your answers

If you finish before time is called, go back to the questions you guessed or omitted to give them further thought. Review other answers if you have time.

10) Return your test materials

If you are ready to leave before others have finished or time is called, take ALL your materials to the monitor and leave quietly. Never take any test material with you. The monitor can discover whose papers are not complete, and taking a test booklet may be grounds for disqualification.

VIII. EXAMINATION TECHNIQUES

1) Read the general instructions carefully. These are usually printed on the first page of the exam booklet. As a rule, these instructions refer to the timing of the examination; the fact that you should not start work until the signal and must stop work at a signal, etc. If there are any *special* instructions, such as a choice of questions to be answered, make sure that you note this instruction carefully.

2) When you are ready to start work on the examination, that is as soon as the signal has been given, read the instructions to each question booklet, underline any key words or phrases, such as *least, best, outline, describe* and the like. In this way you will tend to answer as requested rather than discover on reviewing your paper that you *listed without describing*, that you selected the *worst* choice rather than the *best* choice, etc.

3) If the examination is of the objective or multiple-choice type – that is, each question will also give a series of possible answers: A, B, C or D, and you are called upon to select the best answer and write the letter next to that answer on your answer paper – it is advisable to start answering each question in turn. There may be anywhere from 50 to 100 such questions in the three or four hours allotted and you can see how much time would be taken if you read through all the questions before beginning to answer any. Furthermore, if you come across a question or group of questions which you know would be difficult to answer, it would undoubtedly affect your handling of all the other questions.

4) If the examination is of the essay type and contains but a few questions, it is a moot point as to whether you should read all the questions before starting to answer any one. Of course, if you are given a choice – say five out of seven and the like – then it is essential to read all the questions so you can eliminate the two that are most difficult. If, however, you are asked to answer all the questions, there may be danger in trying to answer the easiest one first because you may find that you will spend too much time on it. The best technique is to answer the first question, then proceed to the second, etc.

5) Time your answers. Before the exam begins, write down the time it started, then add the time allowed for the examination and write down the time it must be completed, then divide the time available somewhat as follows:
   - If 3-1/2 hours are allowed, that would be 210 minutes. If you have 80 objective-type questions, that would be an average of 2-1/2 minutes per question. Allow yourself no more than 2 minutes per question, or a total of 160 minutes, which will permit about 50 minutes to review.
   - If for the time allotment of 210 minutes there are 7 essay questions to answer, that would average about 30 minutes a question. Give yourself only 25 minutes per question so that you have about 35 minutes to review.

6) The most important instruction is to *read each question* and make sure you know what is wanted. The second most important instruction is to *time yourself properly* so that you answer every question. The third most important instruction is to *answer every question*. Guess if you have to but include something for each question. Remember that you will receive no credit for a blank and will probably receive some credit if you write something in answer to an essay question. If you guess a letter – say "B" for a multiple-choice question – you may have guessed right. If you leave a blank as an answer to a multiple-choice question, the examiners may respect your feelings but it will not add a point to your score. Some exams may penalize you for wrong answers, so in such cases *only*, you may not want to guess unless you have some basis for your answer.

7) Suggestions
   a. Objective-type questions
      1. Examine the question booklet for proper sequence of pages and questions
      2. Read all instructions carefully
      3. Skip any question which seems too difficult; return to it after all other questions have been answered
      4. Apportion your time properly; do not spend too much time on any single question or group of questions

5. Note and underline key words – *all, most, fewest, least, best, worst, same, opposite,* etc.
6. Pay particular attention to negatives
7. Note unusual option, e.g., unduly long, short, complex, different or similar in content to the body of the question
8. Observe the use of "hedging" words – *probably, may, most likely,* etc.
9. Make sure that your answer is put next to the same number as the question
10. Do not second-guess unless you have good reason to believe the second answer is definitely more correct
11. Cross out original answer if you decide another answer is more accurate; do not erase until you are ready to hand your paper in
12. Answer all questions; guess unless instructed otherwise
13. Leave time for review

   b. Essay questions
     1. Read each question carefully
     2. Determine exactly what is wanted. Underline key words or phrases.
     3. Decide on outline or paragraph answer
     4. Include many different points and elements unless asked to develop any one or two points or elements
     5. Show impartiality by giving pros and cons unless directed to select one side only
     6. Make and write down any assumptions you find necessary to answer the questions
     7. Watch your English, grammar, punctuation and choice of words
     8. Time your answers; don't crowd material

8) Answering the essay question

Most essay questions can be answered by framing the specific response around several key words or ideas. Here are a few such key words or ideas:

M's: manpower, materials, methods, money, management
P's: purpose, program, policy, plan, procedure, practice, problems, pitfalls, personnel, public relations
   a. Six basic steps in handling problems:
     1. Preliminary plan and background development
     2. Collect information, data and facts
     3. Analyze and interpret information, data and facts
     4. Analyze and develop solutions as well as make recommendations
     5. Prepare report and sell recommendations
     6. Install recommendations and follow up effectiveness

   b. Pitfalls to avoid
     1. *Taking things for granted* – A statement of the situation does not necessarily imply that each of the elements is necessarily true; for example, a complaint may be invalid and biased so that all that can be taken for granted is that a complaint has been registered

2. *Considering only one side of a situation* – Wherever possible, indicate several alternatives and then point out the reasons you selected the best one
3. *Failing to indicate follow up* – Whenever your answer indicates action on your part, make certain that you will take proper follow-up action to see how successful your recommendations, procedures or actions turn out to be
4. *Taking too long in answering any single question* – Remember to time your answers properly

IX. AFTER THE TEST

Scoring procedures differ in detail among civil service jurisdictions although the general principles are the same. Whether the papers are hand-scored or graded by machine we have described, they are nearly always graded by number. That is, the person who marks the paper knows only the number – never the name – of the applicant. Not until all the papers have been graded will they be matched with names. If other tests, such as training and experience or oral interview ratings have been given, scores will be combined. Different parts of the examination usually have different weights. For example, the written test might count 60 percent of the final grade, and a rating of training and experience 40 percent. In many jurisdictions, veterans will have a certain number of points added to their grades.

After the final grade has been determined, the names are placed in grade order and an eligible list is established. There are various methods for resolving ties between those who get the same final grade – probably the most common is to place first the name of the person whose application was received first. Job offers are made from the eligible list in the order the names appear on it. You will be notified of your grade and your rank as soon as all these computations have been made. This will be done as rapidly as possible.

People who are found to meet the requirements in the announcement are called "eligibles." Their names are put on a list of eligible candidates. An eligible's chances of getting a job depend on how high he stands on this list and how fast agencies are filling jobs from the list.

When a job is to be filled from a list of eligibles, the agency asks for the names of people on the list of eligibles for that job. When the civil service commission receives this request, it sends to the agency the names of the three people highest on this list. Or, if the job to be filled has specialized requirements, the office sends the agency the names of the top three persons who meet these requirements from the general list.

The appointing officer makes a choice from among the three people whose names were sent to him. If the selected person accepts the appointment, the names of the others are put back on the list to be considered for future openings.

That is the rule in hiring from all kinds of eligible lists, whether they are for typist, carpenter, chemist, or something else. For every vacancy, the appointing officer has his choice of any one of the top three eligibles on the list. This explains why the person whose name is on top of the list sometimes does not get an appointment when some of the persons lower on the list do. If the appointing officer chooses the second or third eligible, the No. 1 eligible does not get a job at once, but stays on the list until he is appointed or the list is terminated.

X. HOW TO PASS THE INTERVIEW TEST

The examination for which you applied requires an oral interview test. You have already taken the written test and you are now being called for the interview test – the final part of the formal examination.

You may think that it is not possible to prepare for an interview test and that there are no procedures to follow during an interview. Our purpose is to point out some things you can do in advance that will help you and some good rules to follow and pitfalls to avoid while you are being interviewed.

What is an interview supposed to test?

The written examination is designed to test the technical knowledge and competence of the candidate; the oral is designed to evaluate intangible qualities, not readily measured otherwise, and to establish a list showing the relative fitness of each candidate – as measured against his competitors – for the position sought. Scoring is not on the basis of "right" and "wrong," but on a sliding scale of values ranging from "not passable" to "outstanding." As a matter of fact, it is possible to achieve a relatively low score without a single "incorrect" answer because of evident weakness in the qualities being measured.

Occasionally, an examination may consist entirely of an oral test – either an individual or a group oral. In such cases, information is sought concerning the technical knowledges and abilities of the candidate, since there has been no written examination for this purpose. More commonly, however, an oral test is used to supplement a written examination.

Who conducts interviews?

The composition of oral boards varies among different jurisdictions. In nearly all, a representative of the personnel department serves as chairman. One of the members of the board may be a representative of the department in which the candidate would work. In some cases, "outside experts" are used, and, frequently, a businessman or some other representative of the general public is asked to serve. Labor and management or other special groups may be represented. The aim is to secure the services of experts in the appropriate field.

However the board is composed, it is a good idea (and not at all improper or unethical) to ascertain in advance of the interview who the members are and what groups they represent. When you are introduced to them, you will have some idea of their backgrounds and interests, and at least you will not stutter and stammer over their names.

What should be done before the interview?

While knowledge about the board members is useful and takes some of the surprise element out of the interview, there is other preparation which is more substantive. It *is* possible to prepare for an oral interview – in several ways:

1) Keep a copy of your application and review it carefully before the interview

This may be the only document before the oral board, and the starting point of the interview. Know what education and experience you have listed there, and the sequence and dates of all of it. Sometimes the board will ask you to review the highlights of your experience for them; you should not have to hem and haw doing it.

2) Study the class specification and the examination announcement

Usually, the oral board has one or both of these to guide them. The qualities, characteristics or knowledges required by the position sought are stated in these documents. They offer valuable clues as to the nature of the oral interview. For example, if the job involves supervisory responsibilities, the announcement will usually indicate that knowledge of modern supervisory methods and the qualifications of the candidate as a supervisor will be tested. If so, you can expect such questions, frequently in the form of a hypothetical situation which you are expected to solve. NEVER go into an oral without knowledge of the duties and responsibilities of the job you seek.

3) Think through each qualification required

Try to visualize the kind of questions you would ask if you were a board member. How well could you answer them? Try especially to appraise your own knowledge and background in each area, *measured against the job sought*, and identify any areas in which you are weak. Be critical and realistic – do not flatter yourself.

4) Do some general reading in areas in which you feel you may be weak

For example, if the job involves supervision and your past experience has NOT, some general reading in supervisory methods and practices, particularly in the field of human relations, might be useful. Do NOT study agency procedures or detailed manuals. The oral board will be testing your understanding and capacity, not your memory.

5) Get a good night's sleep and watch your general health and mental attitude

You will want a clear head at the interview. Take care of a cold or any other minor ailment, and of course, no hangovers.

What should be done on the day of the interview?

Now comes the day of the interview itself. Give yourself plenty of time to get there. Plan to arrive somewhat ahead of the scheduled time, particularly if your appointment is in the fore part of the day. If a previous candidate fails to appear, the board might be ready for you a bit early. By early afternoon an oral board is almost invariably behind schedule if there are many candidates, and you may have to wait. Take along a book or magazine to read, or your application to review, but leave any extraneous material in the waiting room when you go in for your interview. In any event, relax and compose yourself.

The matter of dress is important. The board is forming impressions about you – from your experience, your manners, your attitude, and your appearance. Give your personal appearance careful attention. Dress your best, but not your flashiest. Choose conservative, appropriate clothing, and be sure it is immaculate. This is a business interview, and your appearance should indicate that you regard it as such. Besides, being well groomed and properly dressed will help boost your confidence.

Sooner or later, someone will call your name and escort you into the interview room. *This is it.* From here on you are on your own. It is too late for any more preparation. But remember, you asked for this opportunity to prove your fitness, and you are here because your request was granted.

What happens when you go in?

The usual sequence of events will be as follows: The clerk (who is often the board stenographer) will introduce you to the chairman of the oral board, who will introduce you to the other members of the board. Acknowledge the introductions before you sit down. Do not be surprised if you find a microphone facing you or a stenotypist sitting by. Oral interviews are usually recorded in the event of an appeal or other review.

Usually the chairman of the board will open the interview by reviewing the highlights of your education and work experience from your application – primarily for the benefit of the other members of the board, as well as to get the material into the record. Do not interrupt or comment unless there is an error or significant misinterpretation; if that is the case, do not hesitate. But do not quibble about insignificant matters. Also, he will usually ask you some question about your education, experience or your present job – partly to get you to start talking and to establish the interviewing "rapport." He may start the actual questioning, or turn it over to one of the other members. Frequently, each member undertakes the questioning on a particular area, one in which he is perhaps most competent, so you can expect each member to participate in the examination. Because time is limited, you may also expect some rather abrupt switches in the direction the questioning takes, so do not be upset by it. Normally, a board member will not pursue a single line of questioning unless he discovers a particular strength or weakness.

After each member has participated, the chairman will usually ask whether any member has any further questions, then will ask you if you have anything you wish to add. Unless you are expecting this question, it may floor you. Worse, it may start you off on an extended, extemporaneous speech. The board is not usually seeking more information. The question is principally to offer you a last opportunity to present further qualifications or to indicate that you have nothing to add. So, if you feel that a significant qualification or characteristic has been overlooked, it is proper to point it out in a sentence or so. Do not compliment the board on the thoroughness of their examination – they have been sketchy, and you know it. If you wish, merely say, "No thank you, I have nothing further to add." This is a point where you can "talk yourself out" of a good impression or fail to present an important bit of information. Remember, *you close the interview yourself*.

The chairman will then say, "That is all, Mr. _____, thank you." Do not be startled; the interview is over, and quicker than you think. Thank him, gather your belongings and take your leave. Save your sigh of relief for the other side of the door.

How to put your best foot forward

Throughout this entire process, you may feel that the board individually and collectively is trying to pierce your defenses, seek out your hidden weaknesses and embarrass and confuse you. Actually, this is not true. They are obliged to make an appraisal of your qualifications for the job you are seeking, and they want to see you in your best light. Remember, they must interview all candidates and a non-cooperative candidate may become a failure in spite of their best efforts to bring out his qualifications. Here are 15 suggestions that will help you:

1) Be natural – Keep your attitude confident, not cocky

If you are not confident that you can do the job, do not expect the board to be. Do not apologize for your weaknesses, try to bring out your strong points. The board is interested in a positive, not negative, presentation. Cockiness will antagonize any board member and make him wonder if you are covering up a weakness by a false show of strength.

2) Get comfortable, but don't lounge or sprawl

Sit erectly but not stiffly. A careless posture may lead the board to conclude that you are careless in other things, or at least that you are not impressed by the importance of the occasion. Either conclusion is natural, even if incorrect. Do not fuss with your clothing, a pencil or an ashtray. Your hands may occasionally be useful to emphasize a point; do not let them become a point of distraction.

3) Do not wisecrack or make small talk

This is a serious situation, and your attitude should show that you consider it as such. Further, the time of the board is limited – they do not want to waste it, and neither should you.

4) Do not exaggerate your experience or abilities

In the first place, from information in the application or other interviews and sources, the board may know more about you than you think. Secondly, you probably will not get away with it. An experienced board is rather adept at spotting such a situation, so do not take the chance.

5) If you know a board member, do not make a point of it, yet do not hide it

Certainly you are not fooling him, and probably not the other members of the board. Do not try to take advantage of your acquaintanceship – it will probably do you little good.

6) Do not dominate the interview

Let the board do that. They will give you the clues – do not assume that you have to do all the talking. Realize that the board has a number of questions to ask you, and do not try to take up all the interview time by showing off your extensive knowledge of the answer to the first one.

7) Be attentive

You only have 20 minutes or so, and you should keep your attention at its sharpest throughout. When a member is addressing a problem or question to you, give him your undivided attention. Address your reply principally to him, but do not exclude the other board members.

8) Do not interrupt

A board member may be stating a problem for you to analyze. He will ask you a question when the time comes. Let him state the problem, and wait for the question.

9) Make sure you understand the question

Do not try to answer until you are sure what the question is. If it is not clear, restate it in your own words or ask the board member to clarify it for you. However, do not haggle about minor elements.

10) Reply promptly but not hastily

A common entry on oral board rating sheets is "candidate responded readily," or "candidate hesitated in replies." Respond as promptly and quickly as you can, but do not jump to a hasty, ill-considered answer.

11) Do not be peremptory in your answers

A brief answer is proper – but do not fire your answer back. That is a losing game from your point of view. The board member can probably ask questions much faster than you can answer them.

12) Do not try to create the answer you think the board member wants

He is interested in what kind of mind you have and how it works – not in playing games. Furthermore, he can usually spot this practice and will actually grade you down on it.

13) Do not switch sides in your reply merely to agree with a board member

Frequently, a member will take a contrary position merely to draw you out and to see if you are willing and able to defend your point of view. Do not start a debate, yet do not surrender a good position. If a position is worth taking, it is worth defending.

14) Do not be afraid to admit an error in judgment if you are shown to be wrong

The board knows that you are forced to reply without any opportunity for careful consideration. Your answer may be demonstrably wrong. If so, admit it and get on with the interview.

15) Do not dwell at length on your present job

The opening question may relate to your present assignment. Answer the question but do not go into an extended discussion. You are being examined for a *new* job, not your present one. As a matter of fact, try to phrase ALL your answers in terms of the job for which you are being examined.

Basis of Rating

Probably you will forget most of these "do's" and "don'ts" when you walk into the oral interview room. Even remembering them all will not ensure you a passing grade. Perhaps you did not have the qualifications in the first place. But remembering them will help you to put your best foot forward, without treading on the toes of the board members.

Rumor and popular opinion to the contrary notwithstanding, an oral board wants you to make the best appearance possible. They know you are under pressure – but they also want to see how you respond to it as a guide to what your reaction would be under the pressures of the job you seek. They will be influenced by the degree of poise you display, the personal traits you show and the manner in which you respond.

ABOUT THIS BOOK

This book contains tests divided into Examination Sections. Go through each test, answering every question in the margin. We have also attached a sample answer sheet at the back of the book that can be removed and used. At the end of each test look at the answer key and check your answers. On the ones you got wrong, look at the right answer choice and learn. Do not fill in the answers first. Do not memorize the questions and answers, but understand the answer and principles involved. On your test, the questions will likely be different from the samples. Questions are changed and new ones added. If you understand these past questions you should have success with any changes that arise. Tests may consist of several types of questions. We have additional books on each subject should more study be advisable or necessary for you. Finally, the more you study, the better prepared you will be. This book is intended to be the last thing you study before you walk into the examination room. Prior study of relevant texts is also recommended. NLC publishes some of these in our Fundamental Series. Knowledge and good sense are important factors in passing your exam. Good luck also helps. So now study this Passbook, absorb the material contained within and take that knowledge into the examination. Then do your best to pass that exam.

EXAMINATION SECTION

EXAMINATION SECTION
TEST 1

DIRECTIONS: Each question or incomplete statement is followed by several suggested answers or completions. Select the one that BEST answers the question or completes the statement. *PRINT THE LETTER OF THE CORRECT ANSWER IN THE SPACE AT THE RIGHT.*

1. In working to establish whether a client is a definite job-counseling case, a counselor's most important clue is 1.____

    A. the counselor's overall evaluation of what the client has said so far, plus an evaluation of nonverbal since the interview started
    B. the feelings, needs, or pressures indicated by the client's words
    C. any comments or recommendations made by a referring professional
    D. the client's statement of her problem

2. Which of the following types of clients would MOST likely be experiencing severe financial problems? 2.____

    A. Culturally different clients
    B. Former military personnel
    C. Displaced homemakers
    D. Voluntary *midlife changers*

3. Which of the following multiple attitude tests is generally considered by job counseling professionals to be the most well-researched? 3.____

    A. Differential Aptitude Test (DAT)
    B. Flanagan Aptitude Classification Test (FACT)
    C. General Aptitude Test Battery (GATB)
    D. Otis-Lennon Mental Ability Test (OLMAT)

4. Approximately what percentage of the job-seeking population knows what they want to do for a living or what jobs match their needs? 4.____

    A. 5-10   B. 20-30   C. 25-40   D. 50-70

5. Which of the following is/are poor choices for an on-the-job tryout? 5.____
    I. An engineering student who is encountering difficulty in choosing among research, applied, sales, and training options
    II. A recent GED recipient who wants to learn about the responsibilities of a paralegal assistant
    III. A high school graduate who wants to learn about the work of a night custodian
    IV. A college graduate with a biology degree who wants to learn about the different types of work in the field of nursing

    The CORRECT answer is:

    A. I, II   B. II, IV
    C. I, III, IV   D. All of the above

1

6. Which of the following statements about newspaper want ads is FALSE? 6.____
They

   A. typically represent hiring by last resort
   B. typically account for about 30–40% of the job leads that result in work
   C. tend to be skewed toward low-paying, high-turnover jobs and highly specialized occupations
   D. are usually the first place job seekers should look for jobs

7. Ideally, any *small talk* that is used to make a job-seeking client comfortable during an initial meeting should be 7.____

   A. of mutual interest
   B. centered on the client
   C. neutral
   D. focused on the counselor

8. Which of the following are significant DISADVANTAGES associated with seeking job search or career advice from employers and other experts? 8.____
   I. Such appearances or interviews rarely lead to concrete job leads and may be considered a waste of time by clients or students.
   II. Unhappy or burned-out advisers may discourage qualified and able applicants.
   III. Each expert is a potential source of personal prejudice.
The CORRECT answer is:

   A. I only
   B. I, II
   C. II, III
   D. All of the above

9. Which of the following questions is considered to be unlawful during a job interview? 9.____

   A. Where do you live?
   B. How old are you?
   C. Which languages other than English are you able to read, write or speak?
   D. Have you ever used another name?

10. Which of the following is NOT a guideline for using want ads in a job search? 10.____

    A. *Apply in person* means an applicant may call if he or she does not own car.
    B. Want ads addresses and phone numbers are usually all right to apply for.
    C. Sunday papers are a good source of want ads for the next week.
    D. It may be a good idea to write one's own *job wanted* ad to let employers know they have skills and want work.

11. Typically, it takes about_____ mass-mailed resumes for a job seeker to get one interview offer. 11.____

    A. 10   B. 70   C. 120   D. 250

12. A counselor often works with clients who are described as *disadvantaged*—a broad term encompassing cultural, educational, environmental, economic, physical, social, and psychological deprivation. Each of the following is typical of the communication pattern of such clients, EXCEPT it is 12.____

    A. temporal rather than spatial
    B. physical and visual rather than auditory
    C. externally oriented, rather than introspective
    D. inductive, rather than deductive

13. Although the Americans With Disabilities Act and most state laws permit employers to use pre-employment medical examinations, they must meet certain requirements. Which of the following is NOT typically one of these?
They

    A. must be applied uniformly to all applicants
    B. must be conducted after an offer of employment is extended
    C. may not include a test for the HIV virus or AIDS
    D. must be job-related

14. Which of the following tests is most appropriate for measuring the readiness of individuals to make choices about vocational issues?

    A. Differential Aptitude Tests (DAT)
    B. Kuder General Interest Survey
    C. Guilford-Zimmerman Survey
    D. Career Development Inventory (CDI)

15. A career professional wants to allow a client to perform a work tryout, but feels that encountering the negative feelings of others employed in the work setting could be very damaging to the client. The counselor's BEST course would be to involve the client in a _____ program.

    A. volunteer work experience
    B. cooperative education
    C. simulated work experience
    D. work-study

16. The MOST commonly used type of educational media in vocational counseling is/are

    A. computer-assisted guidance
    B. programmed instructional materials
    C. printed matter
    D. audio-visual media

17. Which of the following is NOT a significant difference between group career counseling and group career guidance? Group

    A. guidance is only indirectly concerned with attitudes and behaviors
    B. counseling is intended for clients with temporary problems which require more than mere information
    C. guidance procedures can more often be used with large groups
    D. counseling is intended to be instructional; group guidance deals with self-discovery

18. The typical job search involves about _____ rejections for each single offer to be interviewed.

    A. 5   B. 15   C. 30   D. 50

19. According to the Employment and Training ADMINISTRATION'S DICTIONARY OF OCCUPATIONAL TITLES (DOT), which of the following is an operative?

    A. Garbage collector   B. Machinist
    C. Welder   D. Carpenter

20. Which of the following should be avoided when preparing a resume?

    A. Focusing on the needs and aspirations of the job seeker
    B. Writing short sentences and statements
    C. Using examples to illustrate skills or abilities
    D. Using type style, headings, and bullets (•) to accentuate certain elements

21. Which of the following is a personality/attitude assessment that is suggested as appropriate for individuals of college age and older?

    A. Otis–Lennon Mental Ability Test (OLMAT)
    B. Edwards Personal Preference Schedule (EPPS)
    C. Ohio Vocational Interest Survey (OVIS, OVIS II)
    D. Work Values Inventory (WVI)

22. Essentially, there are three major purposes for an initial job seeker/counselor interview. Which of the following is NOT one of these?

    A. Agreeing on the structure and plan for further counseling and related activities
    B. Establishing a relationship so that counseling can continue
    C. Suggesting possible areas of career exploration
    D. Establishing the client's needs and feelings

23. Which of the following is a functional job skill?

    A. Tolerating stress   B. Persistence
    C. Imagination   D. Writing

24. When a client or student names and describes a *dream job,* each of the following is an important response in the early stages of a job search EXCEPT

    A. linking his/her aspirations with immediate, practical steps toward the long–term goal
    B. reinforcing or validating the dream choice
    C. finding out why he/she chose it
    D. cautioning him/her if the job seems outrageous or impractical

25. Educational media in vocational counseling tend to be LEAST effective when

    A. they are introduced carefully and conspicuously into the program
    B. they are applied to small, isolated educational problems
    C. the media developer and the counselor select materials together
    D. they are integrated into the entire program

KEY (CORRECT ANSWERS)

1. A
2. C
3. C
4. B
5. B

6. D
7. A
8. C
9. B
10. A

11. D
12. A
13. C
14. D
15. C

16. C
17. D
18. B
19. C
20. A

21. B
22. C
23. D
24. D
25. B

TEST 2

DIRECTIONS: Each question or incomplete statement is followed by several suggested answers or completions. Select the one that BEST answers the question or completes the statement. *PRINT THE LETTER OF THE CORRECT ANSWER IN THE SPACE AT THE RIGHT.*

1. Which of the following statements about interviewing for a job is TRUE?

    A. A screening interviewer is looking for a reason to accept a candidate, rather than a reason to reject him.
    B. In a nondirective interview, a candidate is permitted to talk about anything he likes.
    C. A candidate should volunteer nothing in a screening interview.
    D. Interviewers will never intentionally introduce stress into an interview situation.

2. Each of the following are disadvantages associated with a holistic life–career planning process EXCEPT

    A. it does not address the important issue of a job seeker's marketable skills
    B. it can overemphasize the nature of individual decision–making
    C. it tends to equate one's worth and life with his work
    D. the possibility of making a poor choice is much more frightening to first–time job seekers

3. When an employer begins to hire and is considering potential employees, she is typically LEAST concerned with

    A. the number of years or months of work experience that is directly related to the position
    B. whether a candidate will be easy to train
    C. whether a candidate will stay on the job after being trained
    D. the quality of a candidate's work habits

4. It is generally agreed that job counselors use standardized tests for a few specific purposes. Which of the following is NOT one of these?

    A. Diagnosis B. Prediction
    C. Placement D. Monitoring

5. In general, 70–90% of employees who are fired from their jobs are let go because

    A. their job skills are poorly matched to the position
    B. they have inappropriate social skills or poor work habits
    C. they have committed one or more serious and costly errors
    D. they cannot handle the workload

6. According to the Employment and Training ADMINISTRATION'S DICTIONARY OF OCCUPATIONAL TITLES (DOT), which of the following is a benchwork occupation?

    A. Bank teller B. Sheet–metal worker
    C. Piano tuner D. Punch press operator

7. Once a job seeker has been taught phone skills, he or she should call each employer _____ before considering the job lead *dead*.

    A. once B. twice
    C. three times D. five times

8. In general, which of the following can be defined as the ultimate outcomes or goals of job search training?
   I. Learning how to find employers by networking and persistence
   II. Selecting a life-long career in the field of one's primary interest
   III. Learning how to describe one's interests and marketable skills in a positive and detailed manner

   The CORRECT answer is:

   A. I only
   B. II only
   C. I, III
   D. All of the above

9. Each of the following is a way in which work experience programs can increase the motivation for learning in disadvantaged clients EXCEPT

   A. developing specific occupational skills
   B. increasing feelings of self-worth
   C. leading to specific job leads
   D. helping clients find the financial assistance needed to remain in school

10. Which of the following is a disadvantage associated with the use of the Flanagan Aptitude Classification Test (FACT) for determining a client's vocational skills?

    A. Test accessories tend to be badly organized and sketchy.
    B. Tests are usually not considered to be interesting or challenging.
    C. The basic assumption of measuring identified job elements and combining test of those basic elements to estimate possible success does not always appear logical.
    D. It is of limited value for clients who are considering occupations that require college preparation.

11. The ideal time for a job seeker to give her resume to a potential employer is

    A. on the first contact, with an explanatory letter
    B. after making an appointment for a personal interview
    C. right at the beginning of a personal interview
    D. after a personal interview

12. Which of the following behaviors is most likely to make an applicant appear overly familiar during an interview?

    A. Raised eyebrows
    B. Shuffling feet
    C. Shrugging
    D. Leaning back

13. Which of the following is an adaptive job skill?

    A. Planning
    B. Analyzing
    C. Being courteous
    D. Memorizing

14. A rule of thumb for resume preparation is that about _____% of the page should remain blank or empty.

    A. 5
    B. 10
    C. 30
    D. 50

15. Each of the following is an important difference between technical and nontechnical skills in the job market EXCEPT

   A. technical skills set the basic requirements for a job
   B. all jobs require a variety of nontechnical skills
   C. nontechnical skills determine success beyond a basic level
   D. all jobs have readily identifiable technical skills

16. The main problem with using printed and audio-visual materials as educational media in job counseling is that they

   A. may move the client too quickly through the job-choice process
   B. retain their usability longer than their accuracy
   C. tend to restrict the role of the counselor
   D. may present too much information to a client at once

17. Which of the following career/job search materials or resources is most likely to be used at the latest phase in the selection process?

   A. Work tryout experience
   B. Printed guidance materials
   C. Interviews with trainers
   D. Computerized materials

18. While many clients have difficulty finding a job right away, some clients fail to find a job at all. Each of the following is usually involved in such a situation EXCEPT

   A. the client is not sure about how to begin an effective job search
   B. there are few to no jobs in the client's particular field of interest or expertise
   C. the client gives up looking for work too soon
   D. the client feels that there are many weak points in his/her past

19. When working with a job seeker who is an ex-offender or drug addict, the BEST course of action is probably to

   A. connect the client to a parole officer or drug counselor who can locate an ex-offender or recovered person who might be interviewed first
   B. contact an advocate from a local office who will strenuously promote the client's job applications
   C. instruct the client to avoid mentioning this aspect of his/her history to potential employers, unless asked about it directly
   D. limit job applications to jobs that involve structured, unskilled tasks

20. During a job interview, an interviewer sometimes appears to be imposing periods of silence. Usually, this is because the interviewer

   A. is testing the candidate to see how he reacts to imposed stress
   B. is manifesting her own confidence in the situation
   C. would like the candidate to elaborate on a response
   D. lacks experience and is formulating the next question

21. When using interest inventories in client exploration, counselors should typically be aware of common problems associated with their application. Which of the following is NOT one of these problems?

    A. Scores may produce a very abbreviated list of suggested occupations.
    B. There are few reliable interest inventories that are keyed directly to occupational options.
    C. The objective information produced by the scores often leads to insufficient counseling.
    D. Clients are often inclined to focus attention on interest scores to confirm their own subjective evaluations, and then move their attention to occupations suggested by those scores.

22. Large group instruction is sometimes used in job search or career education, but it has the significant DISADVANTAGE of

    A. requiring credentialed educators
    B. disseminating large amounts of information to numerous individuals at once
    C. absorbing too much of the client's job search responsibilities
    D. not allowing for group interaction or individual clarification of information

23. A newspaper want ad states that an applicant for a position must have 3–5 years experience in the field. Typically, a client should be encouraged to apply if he has

    A. no experience in the field but is willing to learn
    B. less than one year of experience
    C. one year of experience plus other skills
    D. more than 10 years experience in the field

24. The Strong–Campbell Interest Inventory (SCII) is generally considered to be a useful career–planning tool for each of the following types of job seekers EXCEPT those who

    A. are able to identify some of their likes and dislikes
    B. appear to have some understanding of their career potentials
    C. are considering occupations involving college preparation
    D. appear to be personally confused about the direction their lives are taking

25. Which of the following is NOT an advantage associated with the use of programmed or mechanized materials (workbooks or sequenced exercises) as educational media in job counseling?
    They

    A. allow the client to proceed at a personally determined pace
    B. increase feelings of personalization with each client
    C. assist the client in obtaining information and to process that information in a way that logically moves her toward a decision
    D. assure that specific steps are mastered before advancing to later steps

KEY (CORRECT ANSWERS)

1. C
2. A
3. A
4. C
5. B

6. C
7. C
8. C
9. C
10. D

11. D
12. D
13. C
14. C
15. D

16. B
17. A
18. B
19. A
20. A

21. B
22. D
23. C
24. D
25. B

EXAMINATION SECTION
TEST 1

DIRECTIONS: Each question or incomplete statement is followed by several suggested answers or completions. Select the one that BEST answers the question or completes the statement. *PRINT THE LETTER OF THE CORRECT ANSWER IN THE SPACE AT THE RIGHT.*

1. Which of the following skill, interest, or aptitude tests is untimed?

    A. Otis-Lennon Mental Ability Test (OLMAT)
    B. General Aptitude Test Battery (GATB)
    C. Differential Aptitude Test (DAT)
    D. Guilford-Zimmerman Survey (GZTS)

2. When detailing a specific accomplishment on a resume, a job seeker should FIRST

    A. compare the accomplishment to the performance of others under similar conditions
    B. describe the accomplishment as it was executed
    C. provide information to the reader about the circumstances at the time of the accomplishment
    D. explain how the accomplishment affected the environment in which it was performed

3. Opportunities that put the client in direct contact with work itself are likely to be among the most enlightening of job counseling or training experiences. Which of the following is generally TRUE of these types of experiences? They

    A. usually familiarize the client with the unpleasant parts of a job as well as the potential rewards
    B. can be justified most easily if they are used primarily in the final screenings of the *narrowing* phase of job selection
    C. always involve the client performing at least some work during the experience
    D. tend to involve little time or effort on the part of the employer

4. Which of the following interest inventories is/are keyed directly to occupational options?
    I. Strong-Campbell Interest Inventory (SCII)
    II. Jackson Vocational Interest Survey (JVIS)
    III. Ohio Vocational Interest Survey (OVIS)
    IV. Kuder Occupational Interest Survey – DD (KOIS-DD)

    The CORRECT answer is:

    A. II only   B. I, III   C. I, IV   D. II, III

5. Each of the following is considered to be an important element in any job search training program EXCEPT

    A. reliance on the trainer's personality and skills, rather than a highly structured body of content
    B. provision of support for the job seeker throughout all stages of the job search
    C. training that is situational as well as academic or text-oriented
    D. training that encourages self-sufficiency in the job search

6. A career professional is developing behavioral objectives for a guidance program. The objectives must take each of the following basic elements or criteria into account EXCEPT

   A. client's opportunity to demonstrate behavior
   B. specific characteristics of the client population
   C. expected client performance
   D. evaluative criteria for assessing performance

7. When dealing with *displaced homemakers,* an employment counselor may increasingly encounter women who have decided to leave the home for paid work in order to take on a different role. In which of the following ways does this person differ from the truly displaced homemaker?
   I. The problems of readjusting lifestyles are not as difficult.
   II. Problems with self-concept, independence, and assertiveness are not as frequent.
   III. The decision to go to work is voluntary.

   The CORRECT answer is:

   A. I, II
   B. II *only*
   C. II, III
   D. All of the above

8. In terms of career guidance, which of the following statements about educational media is TRUE?

   A. Media which are only audio are effective if the material presented is unfamiliar to the student.
   B. Usually a combination of media is more effective than any one medium used separately.
   C. They are used primarily to monitor the user's progress.
   D. They offer the user feedback and clarification more reliably than human interaction.

9. _____ diagnosis is a term used to describe the process of determining a job-seeking client's problem or need.

   A. Differential
   B. Dynamic
   C. Decisional
   D. Experience

10. During a job interview, an applicant who claims to have certain skills or work habits should

    A. be prepared to offer 2-3 specific examples of each
    B. compare his or her performance to previous co-workers
    C. focus descriptions on future performance rather than past experience
    D. claim as many as will seem possible to the interviewer

11. Once a job seeker's phone skills are mastered, it should be expected that one interview offer can be gained for every _____ calls.

    A. 1-5
    B. 5-10
    C. 10-20
    D. 20-60

12. Which of the following are most clearly *change* clients?

    A. Culturally unique clients
    B. Young women
    C. Displaced homemakers
    D. Economically disadvantaged clients

13. When using social modeling for behavioral job counseling, which of the following types of models would be considered LEAST effective?

    A. Peers
    B. Models of the opposite sex
    C. Models who are of extremely high status
    D. Models who are similar to the client

14. Which of the following tends to be the LEAST important factor in an employee's experience of job satisfaction?

    A. How a job accommodates an employee's changing identity, values, and needs
    B. How well an employee integrates socially into the work environment
    C. An employee's sense of accomplishment or pride in her work
    D. How well job duties or requirements match the employee's aptitudes

15. All job seekers should be informed of the current estimate that small businesses account for about _____ % of new hiring.

    A. 10-20   B. 25-50   C. 50-70   D. 70-90

16. If a job-seeking client seems hesitant or nervous at the outset of a first meeting, it is MOST appropriate for the counselor to engage in some informal discussion that is

    A. of mutual interest   B. client-centered
    C. neutral   D. counselor-centered

17. In the typical job search, it takes about _____ interviews to get a single job offer.

    A. 5   B. 10   C. 20   D. 40

18. Which of the following is NOT a general rule for preparing a resume?

    A. When describing previous work experience, choose the highest and most general-sounding job title.
    B. Write statements and descriptions all the way across the width of the page.
    C. Use lightly covered, heavy-stock paper.
    D. Place education last if it is not recent.

19. After an employer has addressed a group of clients or helped conduct a seminar in interviewing, the seminar leader should follow up with a solicitation of feedback from the guests. Which of the following questions would typically be asked FIRST in such a post-appearance survey?

    A. Compared to people the employer has interviewed for jobs, what was this student's greatest asset?
    B. Would the employer be willing to do this again?
    C. Did the employer feel as if she helped the student?
    D. Did the student display good hygiene and grooming?

20. Which of the following questions, if asked by an interviewer during a job interview, is considered to be most appropriate and defensible?

    A. Have you ever been arrested?
    B. Will you please list all organizations, clubs, and societies to which you belong?
    C. What is your native language?
    D. Do you have any physical condition or handicap that may limit your ability to perform the job?

21. If a job-seeking client's present possibilities are inadequate or unpromising for future development, he is considered a *change case.* Which of the following should be an initial counseling objective for meeting the client's expressed or inferred need?

    A. Searching for structure to replace confusion
    B. Encouraging a decision or commitment
    C. Removing obstacles that block possible avenues of choice
    D. Making a comprehensive survey of possibilities

22. Which of the following career/job search information resources is considered to be a secondary source?

    A. Programmed materials
    B. Interviews with workers
    C. Site visits
    D. Interviews with supervisors

23. When conducting a training seminar, each of the following is considered to be an appropriate practice EXCEPT

    A. asking open-ended questions
    B. presenting information mostly in objectively-stated facts or observations
    C. concealing the limits of one's own knowledge in order to maintain authority
    D. presenting information in small amounts

24. Typically, the FIRST phase of a client's job search involves

    A. identification of the client's own *job market*
    B. helping the client to sell himself or herself to prospective employers
    C. developing and clarifying self-understanding
    D. connecting the client to other professionals or advisers who may be helpful in the search

25. Which of the following is NOT a problem typically associated with computer-assisted job guidance?

    A. Clients tend to spend too much time with counselors.
    B. The amount of data involved may be overwhelming.
    C. The decision-making process is often not clearly understood.
    D. The role of the counselor is often unclear.

KEY (CORRECT ANSWERS)

1. D
2. C
3. A
4. C
5. A

6. B
7. B
8. B
9. A
10. A

11. C
12. C
13. B
14. D
15. C

16. A
17. A
18. B
19. D
20. D

21. C
22. A
23. C
24. C
25. A

TEST 2

DIRECTIONS: Each question or incomplete statement is followed by several suggested answers or completions. Select the one that BEST answers the question or completes the statement. *PRINT THE LETTER OF THE CORRECT ANSWER IN THE SPACE AT THE RIGHT.*

1. In a vocational guidance program, programmed instructional materials

    A. dictate the pace at which the client can move through the program
    B. record large, summary steps toward goals
    C. provide feedback on the accuracy of client responses
    D. do not require the client to actively respond to messages

    1.____

2. A work experience program, if carefully planned, can eliminate each of the following potential effects EXCEPT

    A. providing a limited view of only one occupation
    B. lacking relationship to a school experience
    C. being negatively influenced by others in the work setting
    D. causing the client to change his or her mind about a possible field of work

    2.____

3. Which of the following behaviors is considered positive and appropriate for a candidate during a job interview?

    A. Hands at sides
    B. Leaning slightly forward
    C. Lowered eyebrows
    D. Arms crossed in front

    3.____

4. During a first meeting with a job-seeking client, the counseling professional must be on the lookout for *presenting statements* that give clues about the client's needs. Which of the following most clearly indicates that the client is primarily a career counseling case?

    A. I want to be sure I'm going into the right field.
    B. My spouse and I have split up.
    C. Someone said I should take a test here.
    D. Every time I'm fired, I'm told to get some counseling.

    4.____

5. Which of the following is NOT a common problem experienced by job seekers during an interview with a potential employer?

    A. Giving answers that have little to do with the question asked
    B. Appearing *job coached* — mastering pat answers that do not fit the individual's job history
    C. Asking too many questions of the interviewer
    D. Stating one's qualifications in a body language and voice that do not match

    5.____

6. Which of the following is typically TRUE of working with rural clients?

    A. Programs should provide maximum group work.
    B. Most do not want to migrate to urban population centers.
    C. Most schools or municipalities have at least one guidance counselor.
    D. They tend to have a more fanciful vision of vocational opportunities.

    6.____

7. Which of the following is NOT an advantage associated with the use of group counseling?
It

   A. encourages clients to seek individual assistance
   B. spreads the effect of the counselor to a number of students
   C. enables clients to become more self-reliant
   D. integrates the social setting into learning

8. Which of the following is a work-oriented technical skill?

   A. Keyboarding
   B. Critical thinking
   C. Problem solving
   D. Perceptiveness

9. For job seekers, the greatest potential source of information about specific jobs and careers are usually

   A. librarians
   B. professional career counselors
   C. employees in the field
   D. employers in the field

10. In general, most career professionals consider it initially more effective to submit a letter to a potential employer, rather than a resume. Which of the following is NOT a reason for this?

    A. Most everybody else sends resumes, making it difficult to get noticed.
    B. There are less established mechanisms within companies for dealing with personally addressed letters.
    C. A resume is more difficult to compose than a letter.
    D. A letter allows the client to focus on strengths in terms of the position, rather than give a comprehensive work history.

11. Which of the following newspaper want ads is most likely to indicate a legitimate job lead?

    A. Earn $70,000 To Start. Learn while you earn. Go as far as you can based on your energy and ability
    B. File Clerks. Exp preferred but not required. Ph. J. Stone for appt. Mutual Life Ins.
    C. Need Extra Money for Christmas? Part time evenings work 6-9. Salary with incentive.
    D. *Closers.* Leads provided. Earn 1000+ weekly. Call Ms. Jones

12. When working with clients who are young women, a job counselor must take special care when using _____ to be alert for possible gender bias.

    A. interest inventories
    B. mentors
    C. work tryout experiences
    D. aptitude tests

13. At the end of a first meeting, a job counselor might ask the client to summarize the main points of the session. Which of the following is NOT a potential disadvantage associated with this approach?
The

A. client may be uncertain about the amount of detail to include
B. client may repeat factual matter rather than feelings and attitudes
C. counselor may unknowingly be encouraging a greater degree of client dependence
D. counselor may not have an opportunity to recheck her conclusions about the client's attitudes or understanding

14. Which of the following is TRUE of a screening interview?

    A. Screening interviewers typically know every detail about the position for which the candidate is interviewing.
    B. A candidate's personality is generally of little importance in a screening interview.
    C. Screening interviewers are not typically trained in interview methodology.
    D. The screener is preoccupied mostly with finding the best person for the position.

15. The creative or functional resume should be used for each of the following situations EXCEPT when

    A. the applicant is changing careers
    B. dates could be interpreted negatively
    C. the applicant is contacting a conservative establishment
    D. the applicant has limited work experience

16. If group therapy is to be used as part of a job counseling program, it is important to remember that it

    A. must involve a fairly large group
    B. is not designed to produce a personality change
    C. must be short-term in duration in order to be effective
    D. must be conducted by a therapist with considerable psychological training

17. During the job search, each of the following is considered appropriate support to be provided by instructors or job-search counselors EXCEPT

    A. technical support for developing resumes, applications, and localized job-seeking tactics
    B. phone banks or access to phones and employer listings
    C. proofreading and typing services for resumes, queries, and applications
    D. material support such as stamps, paper, copying, and a message center for those without phones

18. Which of the following is NOT a strategy recommended by most career professionals for a job seeker to keep an interviewer's attention?

    A. Telling a joke, if one has heard a good one lately
    B. Varying the tone of one's voice
    C. Asking a few superficial personal questions, to get the interviewer to talk about herself
    D. Varying the tempo at which one speaks

19. According to the Employment and Training ADMINISTRATION'S DICTIONARY OF OCCUPATIONAL TITLES (DOT), which of the following is a structural work occupation?

    A. Chimney sweep
    B. Automobile mechanic
    C. Tailor
    D. Forklift operators

20. Probably the most important goal of a work experience program would be to 20.____

    A. select an educational program appropriate for career objectives
    B. develop the client's understanding of the relationships between the world of work and education, which will help the client to contribute to society
    C. appreciate the value of an education
    D. relate interests, abilities, and ambitions to occupational goals

21. According to most employers who conduct interviews, an interview decision is based most significantly on the applicant's 21.____

    A. named job skills   B. body language
    C. clothes and grooming   D. age or gender

22. If a candidate for a job encounters an uncomfortable period of silence during a directive interview, the BEST thing for the candidate to do is to 22.____

    A. retract the previous response
    B. wait for the interviewer to break the silence
    C. elaborate on the previous response
    D. make a lighthearted joke

23. Each of the following is a guideline for using want ads in a job search EXCEPT: 23.____

    A. Want ads should be read completely, from beginning to end, in order to make sure nothing was missed
    B. Job seekers should try to get a copy of an afternoon paper to find jobs opening the next day
    C. Short want ads that don't offer much information should be skipped, because it usually means they are hiding something bad about the job
    D. Most employers write want ads for the ideal employee, and tend to overstate required skills

24. As an educational medium for use in vocational guidance, printed matter 24.____

    A. is not as successful as other media for arousing interest
    B. are rarely used by clients of high educational achievement
    C. is not that useful for disseminating information
    D. has the advantage of staying current long after others have become outdated

25. Which of the following statements about behavioral job counseling is FALSE? 25.____

    A. It may use the strategy of reinforcement.
    B. The effectiveness of vocational counseling is determined by the position the client earns.
    C. It may use the technique of counterconditioning in order to reduce anxiety.
    D. It may try to teach the client through imitating the behavior of another.

KEY (CORRECT ANSWERS)

1. C
2. D
3. B
4. A
5. C

6. B
7. C
8. A
9. D
10. B

11. B
12. A
13. D
14. B
15. C

16. D
17. C
18. A
19. A
20. B

21. C
22. B
23. C
24. A
25. B

EXAMINATION SECTION
TEST 1

DIRECTIONS: Each question or incomplete statement is followed by several suggested answers or completions. Select the one that BEST answers the question or completes the statement. *PRINT THE LETTER OF THE CORRECT ANSWER IN THE SPACE AT THE RIGHT.*

1. Studies show that handicapped persons rehabilitated under the state-federal vocational rehabilitation program repay in Federal income taxes *alone* the Federal government's ENTIRE investment in their rehabilitation within _____ year(s).

    A. one   B. three   C. six   D. ten

2. It is estimated that the number of individuals added to those who need vocational rehabilitation services each year in the United States approximates

    A. 50,000   B. 250,000   C. 1,000,000   D. 25,000,000

3. National *Employ the Physically Handicapped Week* is USUALLY observed during the month of

    A. February   B. May   C. August   D. October

4. The one of the following of the Federal aid programs of public assistance which was MOST recently developed is aid to

    A. citizens over 65 years of age not covered by social security
    B. dependent children
    C. permanently and totally disabled individuals
    D. the blind

5. The one of the following providing placement services for the physically handicapped which restricts its activities to veterans is

    A. Federation Employment Service
    B. Fifty-two Association
    C. Just-One-Break Committee
    D. Vocational Advisory Service

6. The one of the following hospitals which does NOT have a full physical medicine and rehabilitation service with a complete rehabilitation *team* is

    A. Bellevue   B. Bird S. Coler
    C. Goldwater Memorial   D. James Ewing

7. Of the following programs of services to the physically handicapped, the one which is a division of the State Department of Education is

    A. Governor's Committee on Employment of the Physically Handicapped
    B. State Rehabilitation Hospital
    C. Vocational Rehabilitation
    D. Workmen's Compensation

8. The one of the following which constitutes the LARGEST professional group in the National Rehabilitation Association is

   A. counselors
   B. occupational therapists
   C. physical therapists
   D. physicians

9. Three of the following conduct vocational training services for the handicapped. The one which does NOT is

   A. Altro Workshops
   B. American Rehabilitation Committee
   C. The Institute of Physical Medicine and Rehabilitation
   D. The Lighthouse

10. The one of the following that has a sheltered workshop IN ADDITION TO its other rehabilitation facilities is

    A. Bellevue Hospital Physical Medicine and Rehabilitation Service
    B. Hospital for Special Surgery
    C. Institute of Physical Medicine and Rehabilitation
    D. Institute for the Crippled and Disabled

11. The one of the following agencies that does NOT provide direct services to the handicapped is the

    A. American Rehabilitation Committee
    B. Federation of the Handicapped
    C. Goodwill Rehabilitation Committee
    D. International Society for the Welfare of Cripples

12. Of the following agencies, the one which is PARTICULARLY known for its program of rehabilitation for the tuberculous is the

    A. Altro Workshops
    B. Brooklyn Bureau of Social Service
    C. Federation of the Handicapped
    D. Goodwill Industries

13. Of the following agencies, the one which does NOT provide vocational counseling services for the physically handicapped is the

    A. Bureau of Social Services
    B. Federation Employment Service
    C. Fountain House
    D. Just-One-Break Committee

14. The one of the following publications which would be LEAST likely to be of professional interest to a rehabilitation counselor is

    A. COMEBACK
    B. JOURNAL OF REHABILITATION
    C. JOURNAL OF THE ASSOCIATION FOR PHYSICAL AND MENTAL REHABILITATION
    D. PERFORMANCE

15. Each municipal hospital which has a department of physical medicine and rehabilitation has a *rehabilitation team.*
The one of the following occupations which is NOT represented on that team is

A. bracemaker
B. physiatrist
C. psychologist
D. recreation leader

16. Of the following, the one which is NOT considered to be a medical center is

A. Beekman-Downtown
B. Columbia-Presbyterian
C. New York-Cornell
D. New York University-Bellevue

17. The National Institutes of Health are a part of the

A. Kellogg Foundation
B. National Research Council
C. Rockefeller Foundation
D. U.S. Public Health Service

18. Results of I.Q. tests are used as predictors of all of the following EXCEPT

A. learning disabilities
B. educational achievement
C. job performance
D. athletic ability

19. The index usually used to describe an individual's relative mental brightness is

A. C.A.
B. E.Q.
C. I.Q.
D. M.A.

20. Of the following, the BEST criterion of an individual's normalcy is his

A. educational goals
B. interpersonal relationships
C. moral values
D. physical standards

21. The one of the following which has been greatly expanded by federal legislation is the

A. counseling services for disabled veterans provided by the Veterans Administration
B. federal-state vocational rehabilitation program
C. rehabilitation training activities of the Children's Bureau
D. selective placement activities of the various state employment services

22. The one of the following who would be LEAST likely to qualify for services under the federal-state vocational rehabilitation program is a

A. college student paralyzed by poliomyelitis
B. migratory worker stricken by multiple sclerosis
C. self-employed man, fifty years of age, disabled by arthritis
D. worker suffering from an amputation as a result of an industrial accident

23. Of the following, the present policy governing provision of medical services by the Veterans Administration to veterans with non-service connected disabilities is that

A. if a veteran cannot afford to pay for medical care, and if a bed is available, he can receive in-patient care
B. if a veteran cannot afford to pay for medical care, he can receive out-patient care
C. in-patient care can be given only to those with tuberculosis
D. out-patient care can be given only to those with psychiatric problems

24. In terms of vocational rehabilitation, the MOST important area of information which the counselor must know about the patient is his 24.___

    A. educational achievement
    B. expressed goal
    C. previous job experience
    D. type of military service discharge

25. The type of counseling MOST likely to benefit a patient who is still unable to accept his disability two years after injury has occurred is 25.___

    A. educational   B. personal   C. social   D. vocational

KEY (CORRECT ANSWERS)

1.	B	11.	D
2.	B	12.	A
3.	D	13.	C
4.	C	14.	C
5.	B	15.	A
6.	D	16.	A
7.	C	17.	D
8.	A	18.	D
9.	C	19.	C
10.	D	20.	B

21. B
22. B
23. A
24. B
25. B

TEST 2

DIRECTIONS: Each question or incomplete statement is followed by several suggested answers or completions. Select the one that BEST answers the question or completes the statement. *PRINT THE LETTER OF THE CORRECT ANSWER IN THE SPACE AT THE RIGHT.*

1. The development of objective criteria for measuring the physical capacities of patients is MOST difficult in cases of 1.____

    A. coronary heart disease
    B. multiple sclerosis
    C. poliomyelitis
    D. rheumatoid arthritis

2. The prognosis for vocational rehabilitation is LEAST favorable in cases of 2.____

    A. amputation of both upper extremities
    B. diabetes
    C. hemiplegia
    D. muscular dystrophy

3. The term used for a medical specialist in *physical medicine and rehabilitation* is 3.____

    A. orthopedist
    B. physiatrist
    C. physical therapist
    D. physiotherapist

4. It is *generally* accepted that the sense through which people learn MOST readily is the 4.____

    A. auditory   B. kinesthetic   C. tactile   D. visual

5. An obturator is FREQUENTLY used with persons afflicted with 5.____

    A. aphasia
    B. cleft palate
    C. lisping
    D. stuttering

6. Visual acuity of *20/200 or less* is USUALLY interpreted as 6.____

    A. ability to discriminate between light and dark
    B. complete blindness
    C. remediable with glasses
    D. industrial blindness

7. Of the following, the BEST means for testing hearing ability is the 7.____

    A. audiometer
    B. hearing aid
    C. medical examination of the ear
    D. watch tick test

8. Recent studies indicate that adults suffering from a hearing loss, when compared to those with normal hearing, are *usually* MORE 8.____

    A. aggressive   B. intelligent   C. shy   D. stable

9. The perception of one's own muscular movement is called 9.____

    A. cataplasia
    B. kinesthesia
    C. synesthesia
    D. none of the above

10. The one of the following types of speech disorders which will *usually* respond to therapy and retraining in the SHORTEST time is

    A. articulatory disorders
    B. cleft palate speech
    C. post-laryngectomy speech
    D. stuttering

11. As a result of medical care advances, there has been, within recent years, a lessening of the need for rehabilitation counseling services in hospitals for patients with

    A. amputations
    B. arthritis
    C. hemiplegia
    D. tuberculosis

12. The one of the following conditions which is NOT characterized by an orthopedic involvement is

    A. amputations
    B. congenital club foot
    C. diabetes
    D. scoliosis

13. The use of isonicotinic hydrazides in connection with other forms of therapy is a RECENT development in the treatment of

    A. arthritis
    B. cerebral palsy
    C. muscular dystrophy
    D. tuberculosis

14. The one of the following diseases in which insulin is used as a method of medical control and management is

    A. diabetes
    B. epilepsy
    C. rheumatic fever
    D. syphilis

15. The one of the following with which aphasia is MOST commonly associated is

    A. hemiplegia   B. monoplegia   C. paraplegia   D. quadraplegia

16. The kind of patient with which a rehabilitation counselor in a municipal hospital would come into professional contact LEAST frequently is the

    A. geriatric   B. neurologic   C. orthopedic   D. psychiatric

17. In the development of the embryo, the month after which the central nervous system, origin of overt human behavior, is well under way is the

    A. second   B. fifth   C. seventh   D. ninth

18. Three of the following symptoms are frequently associated with multiple sclerosis. The one which is NOT is

    A. metabolic disturbances
    B. speech difficulties
    C. stumbling gait
    D. visual disturbances

19. Of the following, the term which does NOT describe a type of cerebral palsy is

    A. amebiasis   B. ataxic   C. athetoid   D. spastic

20. Three of the following diseases are frequently progressive in the chronic stages. The one which is NOT is

    A. multiple sclerosis
    B. muscular dystrophy
    C. Parkinson's disease
    D. poliomyelitis

21. Three of the following are diseases usually classified as chronic neurological diseases. 21.____
    The one which does NOT fall into this category is

    A. cerebral palsy   B. multiple sclerosis
    C. muscular dystrophy   D. rheumatism

22. The one of the following books that should be of MOST interest to the cerebral palsied is 22.____

    A. BORN THAT WAY by Earl R. Carlson
    B. IT WAS NOT MY OWN IDEA by Robinson Pierce
    C. TRIUMPH CLEAR by Lorraine L. Beim
    D. WHO WALK ALONE by Perry Burgess

23. In general, the percentage of patients stricken with poliomyelitis who will be severely disabled is *approximately* 23.____

    A. 20%   B. 45%   C. 75%   D. 90%

24. With the development of anticonvulsant drugs, the percentage of persons with epilepsy 24.____
    whose seizures can now be completely controlled is *approximately*

    A. 10%   B. 33%   C. 50%   D. 75%

25. The one of the following diseases which affects the SMALLEST number of persons is 25.____

    A. arteriosclerosis   B. congenital heart disease
    C. hypertension   D. rheumatic fever

26. Recent advances in the research and treatment of epilepsy have resulted from the development and widespread use of the 26.____

    A. electrocardiograph   B. electroencephalograph
    C. electromyograph   D. electronic microscope

27. The one of the following books that should be MOST interesting to parents of a congenital amputee is 27.____

    A. AND NOW TO LIVE AGAIN by Betsy Barton
    B. OUT ON A LIMB by Louise Baker
    C. THE CHILD WHO NEVER GREW by Pearl Buck
    D. TRIUMPH OF LOVE by Leona Bruckner

28. The one of the following responsible for the GREATEST number of patients in mental 28.____
    hospitals is

    A. drug addiction   B. paresis
    C. schizophrenia   D. senile dementia

29. Of the following, the LEAST important factor in counseling a patient with a unilateral BK 29.____
    amputation is

    A. diagnosis
    B. etiology
    C. site of amputation
    D. type of prosthetic device worn

30. One of the MOST comprehensive references on the psychological aspects of the physi- 30.___
    cally disabled is that compiled by
    A. Bitner   B. Garrett   C. Kessler   D. Zohl

KEY (CORRECT ANSWERS)

1. A	16. D
2. D	17. A
3. B	18. A
4. D	19. A
5. B	20. D
6. D	21. D
7. A	22. A
8. C	23. A
9. B	24. C
10. A	25. B
11. D	26. B
12. C	27. D
13. D	28. C
14. A	29. D
15. A	30. B

CORRECTION SCIENCE

EXAMINATION SECTION
TEST 1

DIRECTIONS: Each question or incomplete statement is followed by several suggested answers or completions. Select the one that BEST answers the question or completes the statement. *PRINT THE LETTER OF THE CORRECT ANSWER IN THE SPACE AT THE RIGHT.*

1. The one of the following techniques that would NOT be helpful in a correctional program to raise the achievement level of school dropouts is to 1.____

   A. praise all work even if it is not merited
   B. encourage recognition by the peer group
   C. use money as the general reinforcer when appropriate
   D. provide programmed instruction

2. Test validity is BEST described as 2.____

   A. the extent to which a test measures what it was designed to measure
   B. an index of reliability determined by correlating the scores of individuals on one form of a test with their scores on another form
   C. the degree to which a test measures anything consistently
   D. a mathematical index of the extent to which examinees believe an examination to be an appropriate testing instrument

3. The one of the following which is NOT characteristic of traditional learning methods such as lectures, textbooks, films, television, records, and tapes is that 3.____

   A. the learner tends to be passive
   B. the learner may not get deeply involved in the learning process
   C. these methods prove invariably dull
   D. these methods are well adapted to the learning of new concepts

4. The one of the following which would be MOST relevant to a decision concerning whether a particular occupation should be included in a vocational training program is the 4.____

   A. number of people currently employed in the occupation
   B. growth rate of the occupation in the recent past
   C. projected average annual openings in the occupation
   D. job turnover rate in an occupation through death or retirement

5. Following are three statements about the use of correspondence courses for inmates: 5.____
   I. Practical courses such as agriculture, but not cultural courses, are adaptable to correspondence courses.
   II. Correspondence courses provide material for advanced courses in which too few inmates are interested to justify the organization of classes.
   III. One drawback of offering correspondence courses to inmates is that these students often do not make a proper selection of courses.

   Which one of the following *correctly* classifies the above statements?

A. I and II are generally correct, but III is not.
B. II and III are generally correct, but I is not.
C. I is generally correct, but II and III are not.
D. II is generally correct, but I and III are not.

6. The one of the following which is of LEAST value in assessing the effectiveness of a training program for staff is

   A. change in the staff's knowledge
   B. the staff's feelings about the value of the program
   C. changes in the staff's attitudes or values
   D. the degree of success with clients by staff after they have completed the program

7. The one of the following which would be the MOST important factor in insuring that the participants successfully complete a training program is to

   A. increase the time allowed for training
   B. carefully select the trainees
   C. be sure that the material used in the course is readily available to the participants
   D. select instructors who are familiar with the material

8. Which of the following is a CORRECT statement regarding any significant proposed change in correctional practices such as the introduction of work-release programs?

   A. Costs of an innovation must be equal to or less than those of the present system.
   B. Recidivism is a minor factor when planning changes in correctional programs.
   C. Evidence must be provided that public protection is not diminished by the innovation.
   D. A change affecting the entire state system must be reviewed by the federal government.

9. The one of the following statements concerning the characteristics of offenders which is CORRECT is that offenders

   A. are seldom educationally handicapped
   B. tend to have stable work records
   C. usually have little self-esteem
   D. usually have a vocational skill

10. The one of the following that would be MOST helpful to an offender prior to his parole to prepare him to reenter the community is

    A. attendance at prerelease classes in penitentiaries
    B. prerelease visits by parole officers to the offender in the institution
    C. assignment to half-way houses for a period of time prior to release
    D. prerelease visits by parole officers to the family of the offender

11. The selection of a vocational skill to be taught in a training course should be made carefully.
    Of the following, the MOST important factor to consider when making the selection is the

    A. inherent interest of the program's content
    B. simplicity of the skill to be taught

C. attitude of society toward the institution
D. need for the skill in the community

12. The one of the following which is LEAST likely to be an element of a correctional training program based upon a behavior modification approach is

    A. specifying the desired final performance level
    B. holding a meeting between trainer and trainee to plan an individual program
    C. providing reinforcement of desired behaviors
    D. including factors to motivate the trainee

13. Of all the programs for misdemeanants, the LARGEST number of *innovative* efforts are being made for those dealing with

    A. domestic problems   B. alcoholism
    C. juvenile delinquency   D. gambling

14. Of the following, the LEAST important factor in motivating inmates of limited educational background to complete their high school education is the

    A. use of short, attainable, and measurable educational segments
    B. possibility of obtaining a high school'equivalency instead of obtaining a formal diploma
    C. substantial interpersonal relationship between the teacher and the student
    D. reinforcement of learning through recognition

15. There are several advantages in using televised videotape as a means of instruction. Which of the following is NOT an advantage of this method of teaching?

    A. A great number of viewers, spread over a large geographical area, can be reached.
    B. A variety of instructional materials can be integrated within a single lesson.
    C. It is a completely one-way process with the instructor separated from the students.
    D. The information and instruction, on tape, is available for replay whenever desired.

16. Which of the following statements concerning educational programs in correctional institutions is CORRECT?

    A. The costs of educational programming in the correctional setting are generally higher than in the regular educational systems.
    B. The subjects taught in correctional education programs are generally highly innovative.
    C. The status and priority established for institutional education is commensurate with today's demand for such education.
    D. Inmate teachers have rarely been used in educational programs in correctional institutions.

17. Assume that the goal of one of your training sessions for correctional staff is to make the staff aware of how it feels to be confined in a correctional institution. The training technique BEST suited to attain this goal is

    A. reading relevant literature   B. role playing
    C. panel discussion   D. group discussion

18. Following are three statements concerning programmed-learning textbooks: 18.___
    I. The subject matter is arranged logically and in small steps.
    II. The texts are structured so as to demand less concentration than that required for regular methods of instruction.
    III. If the learner has given an incorrect answer, he is immediately made aware of it so that he may correct it before proceeding with the lesson.
    Which of the following CORRECTLY classifies the above statements?

    A. I, II and III are correct.
    B. I and II are correct, but III is not.
    C. I and III are correct, but II is not.
    D. II and III are correct, but I is not.

19. For management by objectives to be successful, all of the following conditions must be fulfilled EXCEPT 19.___

    A. continuous feedback on managerial performance
    B. constant supervision of employees by supervisors
    C. an intensive training program preceding organizational implementation
    D. superior-subordinate relationships characterized by a high degree of cooperation and mutual respect

20. Which of the following types of programs is LEAST appropriate in a correctional institution? A(n) 20.___

    A. religious program
    B. recreational program
    C. individual counseling program
    D. methadone maintenance program

KEY (CORRECT ANSWERS)

1.	A	11.	D
2.	A	12.	B
3.	C	13.	B
4.	C	14.	B
5.	B	15.	C
6.	B	16.	A
7.	B	17.	B
8.	C	18.	C
9.	C	19.	B
10.	C	20.	D

TEST 2

DIRECTIONS: Each question or incomplete statement is followed by several suggested answers or completions. Select the one that BEST answers the question or completes the statement. *PRINT THE LETTER OF THE CORRECT ANSWER IN THE SPACE AT THE RIGHT.*

1. In a modern "information system," there are two main categories: "standard information," consisting of the data required for operational control, and "demand information," consisting of data which, although not needed regularly or under normal circumstances, must be available when required. Following are four types of data:
   - I. Daily count at a prison
   - II. Number of correctional officers who call in sick each day
   - III. Number of prisoners eligible for release within the next six months in certain categories of offenses
   - IV. Average number of paroles granted per year

   Which of the following CORRECTLY categorizes the above types of data into those which are "standard" and those which are "demand" items?

   A. I and II are standard, but III and IV are demand.
   B. I and III are standard, but II and IV are demand.
   C. III is standard, but I, II and IV are demand.
   D. II is standard, but I, III and IV are demand.

2. The *basis* purpose of a detention home for accused juvenile delinquents should be to

   A. serve as a shelter for dependent or neglected children who are temporarily without a home or parental supervision
   B. hold delinquent youngsters pending a court hearing or transfer to another jurisdiction or program
   C. act as a rehabilitative institution following adjudication
   D. act as a rehabilitation institution prior to adjudication

3. The *majority* of prisoners in jails in the United States are incarcerated because

   A. they are a serious threat to themselves and society
   B. they are too poor to get legal assistance
   C. it would cost the community more if they were released and committed offenses
   D. they are too poor to furnish bail pending trial

4. In an effort to assist defendants in obtaining legal counsel, the courts rely MOST heavily on

   A. the National Association for the Advancement of Colored People
   B. bar associations
   C. lawyers' guilds
   D. legal aid and public defender groups

5. All of the following are characteristics of minimum security prisons EXCEPT

   A. inmates work under general or intermittent supervision
   B. they serve a therapeutic function by creating an environment based upon trust rather than strict control

C. the inmates at these institutions are often engaged in public works activities
D. the work experiences they provide directly relate to those the prisoner will face in the real world

6. In the United States, the LARGEST group of persons held in jail are those arrested for 6.____

   A. drunkenness
   B. disorderly conduct
   C. larceny
   D. drug offenses

7. The systems model of a correctional education program reaches a *visible* stage when 7.____

   A. plans are made
   B. cost is estimated
   C. a search is made for sources of funding
   D. a funding request is granted

8. Of the following, the LOWEST stratum in prison subculture is occupied by 8.____

   A. bank robbers
   B. forgers
   C. drug addicts
   D. sex offenders

9. All of the following are characteristics of most of the institutions for sentenced adult prisoners in the United States EXCEPT that they are 9.____

   A. architecturally antiquated
   B. overcrowded
   C. located within metropolitan areas
   D. too large for effective management

10. A correctional program should have measurable objectives so that its success can be evaluated. 10.____
    Of the following, it would be MOST difficult to measure the

    A. change in attitude toward work and study resulting from participation in a correctional program
    B. percentage of participants who obtain employment after release
    C. sum of money earned in a work release program
    D. change in reading level during an educational program

11. The one of the following which should be developed FIRST in establishing a successful training program is the 11.____

    A. content of the training program
    B. facilities for giving training
    C. qualification requirements for staff
    D. agency goals and programs

12. Which of the following statements BEST describes the present role of the courts in respect to rehabilitation in correctional institutions? The courts are 12.____

    A. ready to abandon their "hands off" policy and take a more active role in institutional affairs
    B. deferring to correctional administrators who have the expertise as well as the responsibility for care, custody and treatment of defendants

C. so busy with backlogs of cases that correctional problems occupy a low priority
D. assuming legal responsibility for institutions located in their jurisdictions

13. All of the following statements concerning the money bail system are correct EXCEPT

    A. under the bail system persons may be confined for crimes for which they are later acquitted
    B. members of organized criminal syndicates have little difficulty in posting bail although they are often dangerous
    C. bail is recognized in the law solely as a method of keeping dangerous persons in jail
    D. the bail system discriminates against poor defendants

14. Daytop Village is a treatment program in the city for

    A. drug offenders
    B. sex offenders
    C. mentally retarded offenders
    D. abused children of offenders

15. In the United States, MOST dollars, manpower, and attention in the correctional field have been invested in

    A. traditional institutional services outside the mainstream of urban life
    B. innovative correctional programming at large state institutions
    C. programs for local jails
    D. community based programs

16. Which of the following is the *single* MOST important source of statistics on crime in the United States today?

    A. FBI Quarterly Review
    B. Uniform Crime Reports of the FBI
    C. Journal of Police Science and Criminal Statistics
    D. Federal Report on Criminal Statistics

17. Reading materials can help correctional staff to better understand the attitudes of inmates toward incarceration. SOUL ON ICE, a penetrating story of one man's reaction to California's prisons, was written by

    A. Malcolm X   B. Huey Newton
    C. Bobby Seale   D. Eldridge Cleaver

Questions 18-20.

DIRECTIONS: Answer Questions 18 through 20 SOLELY on the basis of the following passage:

The basic disparity between punitive and correctional crime control should be noted. The first explicitly or implicitly assumes the availability of choice or freedom of the will and asserts the responsibility of the individual for what he does. Thus the concept of punishment has both a moral and practical justification. However, correctional crime control, though also deterministic in outlook, either explicitly or implicitly considers criminal behavior as the result of conditions and factors present in the individual or his environment; it does not think in terms of free choices available to the individual and his resultant responsibility, but rather in terms of the removal of the criminogenic conditions for which the individual may not be responsible and over which he may not have any control. Some efforts have been made to achieve a theoretical reconciliation of these two rather diametrically opposed approaches but this has not been accomplished, and their coexistence in practice remains an unresolved contradiction.

18. According to the "correctional" view of crime control mentioned in the above passage, criminal behavior is the result of

    A. environmental factors for which individuals should be held responsible
    B. harmful environmental factors which should be eliminated
    C. an individual's choice for which he should be held responsible and punished
    D. an individual's choice and can be corrected in a therapeutic environment

19. According to the above passage, the one of the following which is a *problem* in correctional practice is

    A. identifying emotionally disturbed individuals
    B. determining effective punishment for criminal behavior
    C. reconciling the punitive and correctional views of crime control
    D. assuming that a criminal is the product of his environment and has no free will

20. According to the above passage, the one of the following which is an *assumption* underlying the punitive crime control viewpoint rather than the correctional viewpoint is that crime is caused by

    A. inherited personality traits
    B. poor socio-economic background
    C. lack of parental guidance
    D. irresponsibility on the part of the individual

KEY (CORRECT ANSWERS)

1.	A		11.	D
2.	B		12.	A
3.	D		13.	C
4.	D		14.	A
5.	D		15.	A
6.	A		16.	B
7.	D		17.	D
8.	D		18.	B
9.	C		19.	C
10.	A		20.	D

TEST 3

Questions 1-6

DIRECTIONS: Answer Questions 1 through 6 SOLELY on the basis of the following selection:

Man's historical approach to criminals can be conveniently summarized as a succession of three R's: Revenge, Restraint, and Reformation. Revenge was the primary response prior to the first revolution in penology in the 18th and 19th centuries. It was replaced during that revolution by an emphasis upon restraint. When the second revolution occurred in the late 19th and 20th centuries, reformation became an important objective. Attention was focused upon the mental and emotional makeup of the offender and efforts were made to alter these as the primary sources of difficulty.

We have now entered yet another revolution in which a fourth concept has been added to the list of R's: Reintegration. This has come about because students of corrections feel that a singular focus upon reforming the offender is inadequate. Successful rehabilitation is a two-sided coin, including reformation on one side and reintegration on the other.

It can be argued that the third revolution is premature. Society itself is still very ambivalent about the offender. It has never really replaced all vestiges of revenge or restraint, simply supplemented them. Thus, while it is unwilling to kill or lock up all offenders permanently, it is also unwilling to give full support to the search for alternatives.

1. According to the above passage, revolutions against accepted treatment of criminals have resulted in all of the following approaches to handling criminals EXCEPT

    A. revenge   B. restraint   C. reformation   D. reintegration

2. According to the above passage, society *now* views the offender with

    A. uncertainty   B. hatred   C. sympathy   D. acceptance

3. According to the above passage, the second revolution directed *particular* attention to

    A. preparing the offender for his return to society
    B. making the pain of punishment exceed the pleasure of crime
    C. exploring the inner feelings of the offender
    D. restraining the offender from continuing his life of crime

4. According to the above passage, students of corrections feel that the *lack* of success of rehabilitation programs is due to

    A. the mental and emotional makeup of the offender
    B. vestiges of revenge and restraint which linger in correction programs
    C. failure to achieve reintegration together with reformation
    D. premature planning of the third revolution

5. The above passage *suggests* that the latest revolution will

    A. fail and the cycle will begin again with revenge or restraint
    B. be the last revolution
    C. not work unless correctional goals can be defined
    D. succumb to political and economic pressures

6. The one of the following titles which BEST expresses the *main* idea of the above passage is:

   A. Is Criminal Justice Enough?
   B. Approaches in the Treatment of the Criminal Offender
   C. The Three R's in Criminal Reformation
   D. Mental Disease Factors in the Criminal Correction System

Questions 7-12.

DIRECTIONS: Answer Questions 7 through 12 SOLELY on the basis of the following selection:

In a study by J. E. Cowden, an attempt was made to determine which variables would best predict institutional adjustment and recidivism in recently committed delinquent boys. The results suggested in particular that older boys, when first institutionalized, who are initially rated as being more mature and more amenable to change, will most likely adjust better than the average boy adjusts to the institution. Prediction of institutional adjustment was rendered slightly more accurate by using the variables of age and personality prognosis in combined form.

With reference to the prediction of recidivism, boys who committed more serious offenses showed less recidivism than average. These boys were also older than average when first committed. The variable of age accounts in part for both their more serious offenses and for their lower subsequent rate of recidivism.

The results also showed some trends suggesting that boys from higher socioeconomic backgrounds tended to commit more serious offenses leading to their institutionalization as delinquents. However, neither the ratings of socioeconomic status nor "home-environment" appeared to be significantly related to recidivism in this study.

Cowden also found an essentially linear relationship between personality prognosis and recidivism, and between institutional adjustment and recidivism. When these variables were used jointly to predict recidivism, accuracy of prediction was increased only slightly, but in general the ability to predict recidivism fell far below the ability to predict institutional adjustment.

7. According to the above passage, which one of the following was NOT found to be a significant factor in predicting recidivism?

   A. Age
   B. Personality
   C. Socioeconomic background
   D. Institutional adjustment

8. According to the above passage, institutional adjustment was *more* accurately predicted when the variables used were

   A. socioeconomic background and recidivism
   B. recidivism and personality
   C. personality and age
   D. age and socioeconomic background

9. According to the above passage, which of the following were *variables* in predicting both recidivism and institutional adjustment?   9.____

   A. Age and personality
   B. Family background and age
   C. Nature of offense and age
   D. Personality

10. Which one of the following conclusions is MOST justified by the above passage?   10.____

   A. Institutional adjustment had a lower level of predictability than recidivism.
   B. Recidivism and seriousness of offense are negatively correlated to some degree.
   C. Institutional adjustment and personality prognosis, when considered together, are significantly better predictors of recidivism than either one alone.
   D. A delinquent boy from a lower class family background is more likely to have committed a serious first offense than a delinquent boy from a higher socioeconomic background.

11. The study discussed in the passage found that delinquent boys from a higher socioeconomic background tended to   11.____

   A. commit more serious crimes
   B. commit less serious crimes
   C. show more recidivism than average
   D. show less recidivism than average

12. The *most appropriate* conclusion to be drawn from the study discussed above is that   12.____

   A. delinquent boys from higher socioeconomic backgrounds show less institutional adjustment than average
   B. a high positive correlation was found between recidivism and institutional adjustment
   C. home environment, although not significantly related to recidivism, did influence institutional adjustment
   D. older boys are more likely to commit more serious first offenses and show less recidivism than younger boys

Questions 13-18.

DIRECTIONS: Answer Questions 13 to 18 SOLELY on the basis of the information contained in the following charts and notes.

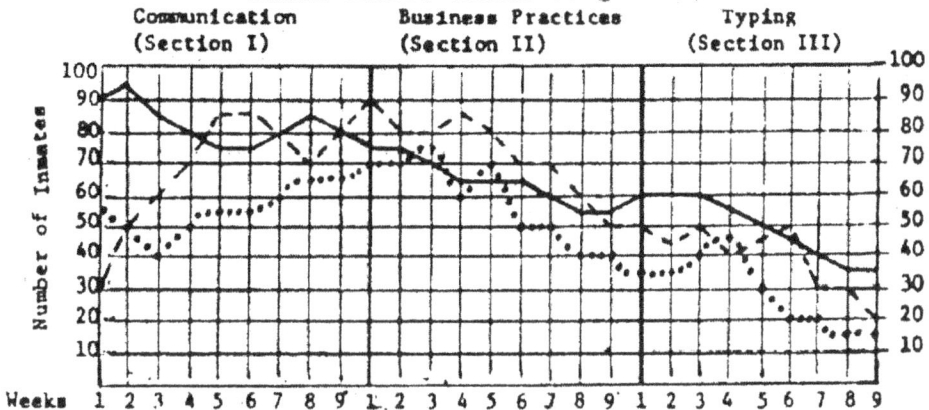

CHART I
Number of Inmates Enrolled in Libertyville's
Basic Office Skills Program

Symbol Crime Category
———   Victimless Crimes
- - - - Crimes Against Property
······· Violent Crimes

NOTES: Inmates can enter a section of the program at any point. Inmates can complete a section of the program at any point by passing an examination.

Enrollment at the end of a section does not necessarily indicate successful completion of that section.

CHART II
Number of Inmates Who Successfully Completed
Each Section of Libertyville's
Office Skills Program

Crime Category	Completed Section I	Completed	Completed Section III
Victimless Crimes	78	55	37
Crimes Against Property	43	57	28
Violent Crimes	80	50	18

CHART III
Percentage of Recidivism Within First Year of Parole
Among Inmates Who Successfully Completed
Various Stages of Libertyville's
Office Skills Program

Crime Category	Completed Section I	Completed Section II	Completed Section III
Victimless Crimes	40%	30%	15%
Crimes Against Property	30%	15%	5%
Violent Crimes	35%	25%	10%

13. The percentage of inmates who successfully completed Section I and were recidivists is, most nearly,   13.____

    A. 21%   B. 35%   C. 38%   D. 47%

14. The ratio of the number of inmates who started Section III the first week to the number who successfully completed Section III is, most nearly,   14.____

    A. 1.5:1   B. 1.7:1   C. 2.1:1   D. 2.5:1

15. During which of the following weeks of the program was the enrollment by those who committed victimless crimes *exceeded* by both those who committed crimes against property and by those who committed violent crimes?   15.____

    A. Week 1 of the Communication Section
    B. Week 3 of the Business Practices Section
    C. Week 9 of the Business Practices Section
    D. Week 6 of the Typing Section

16. If the average number of inmates enrolled in any stage of the program is considered to be the number of inmates enrolled during week 5 of that Section, what is the difference between the average number of inmates enrolled in Section I and in Section III?   16.____

    A. 90   B. 125   C. 190   D. 215

17. Assume that 60 percent of the inmates who completed Section III of the Office Skills Program enrolled the first week of the program and completed all three sections of the program. The percent of the initial enrollees who completed the ENTIRE Office Skills Program was, most nearly,   17.____

    A. 21%   B. 28%   C. 36%   D. 49%

18. The one of the following periods which exhibits the GREATEST percentage change in enrollment of inmates in the crimes against property category is weeks   18.____

    A. 1 to 2 in the Communication Section
    B. 2 to 4 in the Communication Section
    C. 4 to 6 in the Business Practices Section
    D. 3 to 4 in the Typing Section

19. A recent study of the bail system as it is administered conducted by the Legal Aid Society, concluded that the one of the following factors which has the STRONGEST impact on an accused person's chances of being convicted is   19.____

    A. whether the person is detained or released prior to trial
    B. the weight of evidence against the person
    C. the type and seriousness of the alleged crime
    D. whether the person has a criminal record

20. Of the following, the *chief* DISADVANTAGE of using on-the-job training is that it 20._____
    A. is initially more costly than using other types of training
    B. is often carried on with little or no planning
    C. requires the worker to remain in the environment in which he will be working
    D. prevents the trainee from obtaining the benefits of a professional's experience

KEY (CORRECT ANSWERS)

1.	A	11.	A
2.	A	12.	D
3.	C	13.	B
4.	C	14.	B
5.	C	15.	B
6.	B	16.	A
7.	C	17.	B
8.	C	18.	A
9.	A	19.	A
10.	B	20.	B

EXAMINATION SECTION

TEST 1

DIRECTIONS: Each question or incomplete statement is followed by several suggested answers or completions. Select the one that BEST answers the question or completes the statement. *PRINT THE LETTER OF THE CORRECT ANSWER IN THE SPACE AT THE RIGHT.*

1. Of the following, the BEST source of trend information pertaining to occupational data is
    A. *The U.S. Industrial Outlook*
    B. *Estimates of Worker Trait Requirements*
    C. *Occupational Outlook Handbook*
    D. *Dictionary of Occupational Titles*

    1._____

2. Of non-white youngsters in the United States who drop out before completing four years of high school, what proportion come from families earning less than $20,000?
    A. 25%
    B. 40%
    C. More than 50%
    D. More than 90%

    2._____

3. Educational attainment has been rising. Median institution years of attainment for persons now holding clerical or sales jobs average
    A. more than 12 years
    B. less than 12 years
    C. more than 10 years
    D. less than 10 years

    3._____

4. Automation and technological development are causing job displacement throughout the economy. Which industry sector has suffered the most severe job losses due to these factors?
    A. Services
    B. Agriculture
    C. Manufacturing
    D. Professional, technical and managerial occupations

    4._____

5. *Choosing a Vocation*: Frank Parsons; *Mind That Found Itself*: _____
    A. Ralph Berdie
    B. Carl Rogers
    C. Mary L. Northway
    D. Clifford Beers

    5._____

45

6. The counselor will find which one of the books below extremely valuable　　6._____
   in developing his occupational information program because it contains a
   complete annotated bibliography of career materials—books, pamphlets,
   posters, subscription services, etc.?
   - A. Forrester, *Occupational Literature*
   - B. Roe, *Psychology of Occupations*
   - C. Greenleaf, *Occupations and Careers*
   - D. Shartle, *Occupational Information*

7. The proper sequence of the four occupation categories listed below in　　7._____
   accordance with the number of people employed in each, proceeding
   from highest to lowest, is
   - A. manufacturing; government; wholesale and retail trade; services
   - B. government; manufacturing; services; wholesale and retail trade
   - C. services; wholesale and retail trade; manufacturing; government
   - D. manufacturing; wholesale and retail trade; government; services

8. The vocational guidance movement, which is the parent of current　　8._____
   guidance programs, was spearheaded by
   - A. Frank Parsons
   - B. Clifford Beers
   - C. John Brewer
   - D. Harry Kitson

9. Among the following occupational categories, the one expected to grow　　9._____
   MOST rapidly in the next ten years is that of
   - A. sales workers
   - B. skilled workers
   - C. managers
   - D. clerical workers

10. The largest quantity of occupational information is published by　　10._____
    - A. Science Research Associates
    - B. New York Life Insurance Company
    - C. Chronicle Guidance Publications
    - D. United States Government

11. The only occupational field – outside of farming – which has declined in　　11._____
    actual numbers of employed since the end of World War II has been the
    field of
    - A. printing trades
    - B. tool and die machine work
    - C. building construction
    - D. unskilled jobs

12. One of the effects of automation and productivity has been to
    A. increase the education and training requirements of jobs
    B. eliminate many middlemen in trade and service fields
    C. decrease the number of semi-professional jobs
    D. lower the level of earnings in service jobs

13. Which of the following problems presents the MOST serious challenge to the counselor's skill?
    A. Redirecting the goals of the low-ability, high-aspiration students
    B. Redirecting the goals of the high-ability, low-aspiration students
    C. Changing the direction of a student whose goals are at an appropriate level, but wrongly directed
    D. Encouraging a client to investigate a promising field

14. There are a number of excellent resources for assistance in developing units on vocations. The writings of the specialists vary. Which of the following authors should you recommend on vocation?
    A. Gerald T. Kowitz
    B. Walter Lifton
    C. Robert Hoppock
    D. Gilbert Wrenn

15. Of the following occupational categories, the one that provides jobs to the largest number of people is
    A. craftsmen, foremen and kindred workers
    B. operatives and kindred workers
    C. professional, technical and kindred workers
    D. clerical and kindred workers

16. The *Dictionary of Occupational Titles* has developed a new coding system. Which of the following categories is NOT part of the code?
    A. Data   B. Ideas   C. People   D. Things

17. The most recent edition of the *Dictionary of Occupational Titles* includes all of the following EXCEPT
    A. the outlook for particular occupations in the next five to ten years
    B. bound volumes of occupational listings and descriptions
    C. occupations likely to be found in any industry
    D. training requirements and methods of entry into occupations

18. Most women who take jobs do so because of
    A. financial necessity
    B. desire to escape from boredom at home
    C. personal satisfaction
    D. desire to provide some extra luxuries for the home

4 (#1)

19. The single largest employer of labor in this nation is which of the following industry divisions?   19._____
    A. Manufacturing
    B. Government
    C. Wholesale and retail trade
    D. Construction

20. High school seniors dropping out before graduation are MOST likely to come from a household where the family head is which one of the following?   20._____
    A. White-collar worker
    B. Manual service worker
    C. Farm worker
    D. Unemployed or not in labor force

21. Of the following, the BEST source of fundamental information about job situations and future trend is   21._____
    A. *The Occupation Index*
    B. *Occupational Outlook Handbook*
    C. *Dictionary of Occupational Titles*
    D. *Career Briefs*

22. It was decided recently to screen all potential draftees far before induction. The purpose of this step was to   22._____
    A. increase the number of volunteers
    B. get the unemployed off the streets
    C. get a better picture of the manpower skills available
    D. provide remedial help to people who fail the induction tests

23. The employment picture in our country is in a state of rapid change. In which one of the following states is employment increasing MOST rapidly?   23._____
    A. Illinois   B. Oregon
    C. New York   D. Texas

24. Of the following, which is the correct statement of a current occupational trend?   24._____
    A. The geographic movement of workers is increasing
    B. The population is increasing, but the available labor force is decreasing
    C. The proportion of workers aged 45 and over is decreasing
    D. The proportion of workers providing services is decreasing

25. The manpower outlook in large cities in the years 1980 through 1990 indicated a decline in the
    A. number of persons in the resident labor force under age 25
    B. number of semi-skilled jobs
    C. number of females in the resident labor force
    D. proportion of the population accounted for by non-whites

25._____

KEY (CORRECT ANSWERS)

1. C	11. D	21. B
2. C	12. A	22. D
3. A	13. A	23. D
4. B	14. C	24. A
5. D	15. B	25. B
6. A	16. B	
7. D	17. A	
8. A	18. A	
9. D	19. A	
10. D	20. D	

TEST 2

DIRECTIONS: Each question or incomplete statement is followed by several suggested answers or completions. Select the one that BEST answers the question or completes the statement. *PRINT THE LETTER OF THE CORRECT ANSWER IN THE SPACE AT THE RIGHT.*

1. The term "vocational development" is preferred to that of "vocational choice" by one of the following persons. He claims that in deciding on an occupation, one is choosing a means of implementing a self-concept; he claims, also, that the individual goes through various "life stages" in so doing. He is
    A. Ginzberg
    B. Axelrod
    C. Karnes
    D. Super

   1._____

2. If present trends continue, what percentage of all workers in the U.S. will be women?
    A. 50%   B. 25%   C. 33%   D. 66%

   2._____

3. Which one of the following occupational groups is MOST responsive to rises and falls in the business cycles?
    A. Professionals
    B. Craftsmen and foremen
    C. Semi-skilled workers
    D. Clerical workers

   3._____

4. The more generally used forms of the *Kuder Preference Record—Occupational* contain nine or ten scales, each of which reflects an area or cluster of activity, such as mechanical, social service or clerical. The *Strong Vocational Interest Blank*, on the other hand, is typified by an approach which uses criterion groups of
    A. pre- and post-college individuals whose academic majors, interests and competencies are a clear matter of record
    B. successfully employed men in a variety of occupations whose responses are compared to a presumably representative group of men in general
    C. children at various social-class levels, whose interests and actual careers have been followed up subsequently for more than 25 years
    D. superior and marginal achievers in a large number of professions and sub-professions

   4._____

5. Occupational information which specifies hiring standards is known as the
    A. job specification   B. job description
    C. job analysis   D. occupational analysis

   5._____

6. State Employment Service interviewers classify experienced applicants according to
    A. the job opportunities available
    B. abilities and skills
    C. physical capacities
    D. educational background

7. Related jobs can more easily be located in the *Dictionary of Occupational Titles* in Part
    A. I   B. II   C. III   D. IV

8. Of the following broad areas of work in which people are engaged, the one in which MOST workers are employed is
    A. clerical work
    B. farming
    C. semi-skilled work
    D. selling

9. The proportion of the total working force engaged in certain broad occupational fields has shifted markedly in the period from 1910 to the present. Of the following, the field in which there has been the greatest increase is
    A. farm workers
    B. service workers
    C. laborers
    D. clerks and salespeople

10. Social Security or Old Age and Survivors Insurance is paid for by
    A. taxes deducted from the employee's salary only
    B. funds set aside by the federal government from income taxes
    C. the state in which the worker lives at the time of his retirement or death
    D. taxes deducted from the employee's salary plus an equal amount paid by the employer

11. If a counselor wishes to provide vocational guidance using as one basis an occupational-interest test, he must FIRST be certain the test has _____ validity.
    A. content
    B. predictive
    C. concurrent
    D. construct

12. Strong recently reported that a group of engineers responded to the Vocational Interest Inventory in the same manner as they had 20 years before. We may conclude from this that the test demonstrates adequate
    A. reliability
    B. validity
    C. usefulness
    D. efficiency

12._____

13. One of the major new emphases in vocational counseling which has been stressed by Gilbert Wrenn and others is that
    A. the counselor helps the student define goals, not merely to inventory capacities
    B. more women are going to be working in the future
    C. talent must be looked at in terms of its marketable value
    D. the counselor must stress the fact that satisfying occupations are decreasing

13._____

14. Unemployment has particularly affected the disadvantaged groups. For example, compared with a national average rate of about 6%, unemployment among teenage Puerto Ricans in New York City runs about
    A. 2%   B. 5%   C. 10%   D. 40%

14._____

15. Job mobility is an important factor in labor force dynamics. Which of the following groups has the highest proportion of persons who change their jobs in the course of a year?
    A. Unskilled laborers
    B. Clerical workers
    C. Professional and technical personnel
    D. Sales workers

15._____

16. In Menninger's view, which one of the following factors accounts for the greatest number of job dismissals?
    A. Technical incompetence
    B. Inability to relate to other workers
    C. Inability to relate to authority figures
    D. Poor work habits

16._____

17. Among American industries, there is much variation with regard to the unemployment experience of the workforce. Which one of the following major industry divisions generally has the highest unemployment rate?
    A. Agriculture
    B. Construction
    C. Trade
    D. Manufacturing

17._____

18. The only major industry division which is expected to decline in the next decade is
    A. mining
    B. agriculture
    C. manufacturing
    D. transportation and public utilities

    18._____

19. The incidence of unemployment varies significantly by industry. The highest unemployment rates are found in which American industry division?
    A. Manufacturing
    B. Construction
    C. Trade
    D. Government

    19._____

20. During the next ten years, job opportunities in government, in relation to total labor force growth, is expected to show the following change:
    A. more than average
    B. average
    C. less than average
    D. no change

    20._____

21. Job opportunities are growing fastest in jobs requiring the most education; nevertheless, in 2000, what proportion of the labor force had NOT completed high school?
    A. More than 70 percent
    B. More than 50 percent
    C. More than 30 percent
    D. More than 10 percent

    21._____

22. *Occupational Outlook Handbook* is a publication of the
    A. Vocational Advisory Service
    B. United States Bureau of Labor Statistics
    C. Welfare Council
    D. Vocational Counselors' Association

    22._____

23. What is the general relationship of unemployment rates for non-white and white workers?
    A. Lower for non-whites
    B. About the same
    C. Twice as high for non-whites
    D. Five times as high for non-whites

    23._____

24. Teenagers' unemployment experience, in relationship to the rest of the labor force, is evidenced in an unemployment rate which bears what relationship to the average for all groups?
    A. Three times as high
    B. Twice as high
    C. Fifty percent higher
    D. About the same

25. The highest unemployment rate experienced by any labor force category is found among which ONE of the following groups?
    A. Unskilled laborers
    B. Women
    C. High school dropouts
    D. Non-white teenage girls

KEY (CORRECT ANSWERS)

1. D	11. B	21. C
2. A	12. A	22. B
3. C	13. A	23. C
4. B	14. D	24. A
5. A	15. A	25. C
6. B	16. B	
7. B	17. B	
8. C	18. A	
9. D	19. B	
10. D	20. A	

EXAMINATION SECTION
TEST 1

DIRECTIONS: Each question or incomplete statement is followed by several suggested answers or completions. Select the one that BEST answers the question or completes the Statement. *PRINT THE LETTER OF THE CORRECT ANSWER IN THE SPACE AT THE RIGHT.*

1. While school is in session, from September to June generally, children 14 and 15 years old may not be employed in any occupation (except farm work and selling or distributing newspapers) more than

    A. 4 hours on any school day
    B. 8 hours on Saturday or a non-school day
    C. 27 hours in any week
    D. 5 days in any week

    1.____

2. The number of different jobs in the United States today is approximately

    A. 10,000
    B. 25,000
    C. 75,000
    D. 100,000

    2.____

3. The ratio of men to women in the labor force is approximately two to one (full-time). In which of the following occupational categories would we be MOST likely to find a similar ratio?

    A. Professional and technical
    B. Clerical
    C. Managerial
    D. Proprietary

    3.____

4. The Fair Labor Standards Act pertains to

    A. migrant farm labor
    B. non-discrimination in employment
    C. federal wage and hours
    D. compulsory retirement

    4.____

5. More clerical workers will be needed in the cities over the next few years chiefly because of the

    A. greater urbanization and per capital income
    B. youth who will account for 44% of the increase in the labor force
    C. automation and improvement of office operations
    D. growth of government, finance, and insurance

    5.____

6. During high school and early college years, the occupational preferences of youth tend to

    A. remain essentially stable
    B. change in a small proportion of cases
    C. change in the majority of cases
    D. change in all but a few cases

    6.____

7. The DICTIONARY OF OCCUPATIONAL TITLES is a publication of the 7.___

   A. Psychological Corporation
   B. California Test Bureau
   C. U.S. Government Printing Office
   D. New York City Board of Education

8. JOBS AND FUTURES was a regular feature of the magazine 8.___

   A. SEVENTEEN   B. MADEMOISELLE
   C. PIC   D. VOGUE

9. OCCUPATIONAL OUTLOOK HANDBOOK is a reference work prepared by 9.___

   A. GLAMOUR magazine
   B. Occupational Index, Inc.
   C. United States Department of Labor
   D. Science Research Associates, Inc.

10. Today's National Career Development Association (NCDA) was formerly known as 10.___

    A. New York State Department of Labor
    B. National Vocational Guidance Association
    C. New York Vocational Guidance Association
    D. Vocational Advisory Service

11. The official journal of the National Career Development Association is called 11.___

    A. GUIDANCE INDEX   B. VOCATIONS
    C. GUIDANCE BULLETIN   D. CAREER DEVELOPMENT QUARTERLY

12. Donald E. Super evaluated a number of widely used tests in his book 12.___

    A. APPRAISING VOCATIONAL FITNESS
    B. THE VALUE OF TESTS IN THE GUIDANCE PROGRAM
    C. TESTING AND COUNSELING IN THE JUNIOR HIGH SCHOOL
    D. THE DYNAMICS OF VOCATIONAL GUIDANCE

13. Recent proportions of labor force growth indicate that, in the next ten years, the Nation's labor force will grow each year by about _____ percent. 13.___

    A. 5   B. 2.5   C. 0.6   D. -1.0

14. Since 1981, the unemployment rate in the United States has 14.___

    A. risen substantially
    B. risen slightly
    C. remained about unchanged
    D. declined

15. Workers in certain occupations are more likely than other workers to hold second jobs. The occupational group which shows the HIGHEST rate of second-job holding of those listed is 15.___

    A. clerical workers   B. professionals
    C. sales workers   D. service workers

16. The term "operative" is used by the Census Bureau to describe a group of workers popularly referred to as _____ workers.

    A. semi-skilled
    B. unskilled
    C. service
    D. farm

17. At the present time, the proportion of all jobs in government at the federal, state and local levels is about

    A. 40%   B. 33%   C. 25%   D. 15%

18. Super's APPRAISING VOCATIONAL FITNESS is a book which is mainly concerned with which of the following?

    A. Clinical rather than test methods of vocational appraisal
    B. Vocational tests: their rationale, construction and predictive validity
    C. The Career Pattern Study
    D. The appraisal of personality

19. Wolfbein contends that the increase in education and training requirements for MOST jobs is due to the

    A. upward shift in occupational structure and the increasing complexity of jobs
    B. increased life span and the increased work life of the average worker
    C. relationship of geographic area to occupational opportunity and the increased number of women in the labor force
    D. older age at which individuals enter the labor force and the increase in service oriented occupations

20. Which one of the following job categories is expected to rise MOST rapidly in the current decade?

    A. Managers, officials and proprietors
    B. Service workers
    C. Sales workers
    D. Craftsmen and foremen

21. Over a lifetime of work, differences in earning levels are related to educational attainment. A college degree as compared with a high school diploma can mean a difference of close to what amount on the average?

    A. $50,000
    B. $75,000
    C. $125,000
    D. $300,000

22. Multiple job holding has increased substantially in recent years. Which one of the following groups of workers has the highest rate of dual-job holding?

    A. Farmers
    B. Clerical workers
    C. Professional and technical workers
    D. Private household workers

23. Which one of the following statements is NOT true of generally prevailing attitudes in American society regarding occupations? 23.___

   A. White collar work is superior to manual work.
   B. Working for an established firm is superior to self-employment.
   C. Working for a large firm is superior to working for a small firm.
   D. Clean occupations are superior to dirty ones.

24. Poverty is a matter of increasing concern in this nation. As a rule of thumb, what income for a family of four is considered to be the approximate poverty-level dividing line? 24.___

   A. $15,000 B. $20,000
   C. $26,000 D. $34,000

25. Over the past century, farm employment has been declining, thus releasing thousands of workers to be absorbed by urban industry. During the ten-year period from 1970 to 1980, the nation's farm population 25.___

   A. declined by about 30%
   B. declined by about 10%
   C. remained unchanged
   D. reversed the long-term down trend

KEY (CORRECT ANSWERS)

1.	B	11.	D
2.	B	12.	A
3.	A	13.	C
4.	C	14.	D
5.	D	15.	B
6.	C	16.	A
7.	C	17.	D
8.	B	18.	B
9.	C	19.	A
10.	B	20.	B

21. D
22. A
23. B
24. B
25. A

TEST 2

DIRECTIONS: Each question or incomplete statement is followed by several suggested answers or completions. Select the one that BEST answers the question or completes the statement. *PRINT THE LETTER OF THE CORRECT ANSWER IN THE SPACE AT THE RIGHT.*

1. In recent years, there has been a very substantial increase in part-time workers in the labor force. The Manpower Report of the President concluded that

    A. this has been a major cause of unemployment among full-time workers
    B. it reflects the low level of the nation's economy
    C. part-time workers are found more extensively among the unskilled
    D. the growth in part-time work has permitted greater utilization of the nation's manpower, particularly among women and young people

    1._____

2. Between 1970 and 1980, about 3.5 million male workers were added to the nation's work force. Compared with this total, females added to the work force accounted for

    A. 4.8 million
    B. 3.2 million
    C. 2.1 million
    D. 1.2 million

    2._____

3. Many factors have contributed to the increase in participation of women in the labor force. An important factor has always been, in the case of married women, the income of husband. At what income level of the husband do we find the highest proportion of employed married women?

    A. Under $32,000
    B. $32,000 to $60,000
    C. $60,000 to $80,000
    D. $80,000 and over

    3._____

4. The age chronology of the participation of women in the work force has undergone dramatic change in the last four decades. In what age category do we now find the fastest growth in the proportion of women participating in the labor force?

    A. 14 to 24
    B. 35 to 44
    C. 45 to 54
    D. Over 65

    4._____

5. The importance of women in the nation's work force has been growing steadily. It is now estimated that during a lifetime, of every 10 women, how many will work for pay at one time or another?

    A. 2
    B. 4
    C. 6
    D. 8

    5._____

6. The skilled worker category is expected to grow in importance during the present decade. The major path to employment in such jobs has been predominantly through

    A. on-the-job training
    B. vocational school
    C. military training
    D. formal apprenticeship

    6._____

7. The average person employed in the United States as a clerical or sales worker has had, in the way of formal schooling, what number of years?

    A. 6
    B. $8\frac{1}{2}$
    C. $12\frac{1}{2}$
    D. 14

    7._____

8. During the five years, from 1977 to 1982, the nation's economy reflected growth in some industry sectors, declines in others. Which of the following industry divisions showed the largest gain during this period? 8.___

   A. Trade
   B. Finance, insurance and real estate
   C. Services
   D. Government

9. Of the nation's major industry sectors, which of the following reported the largest absolute employment decline in the last five years? 9.___

   A. Manufacturing   B. Construction
   C. Mining   D. Transportation

10. Here are the names of three volumes: VOCATIONAL INTERESTS OF MEN AND WOMEN; I FIND MY VOCATION; APPRAISING VOCATIONAL FITNESS. Which one of the following authors is NOT represented by these titles? 10.___

    A. Harry Kitson   B. Donald E. Super
    C. Edward K. Strong D. Frederic Kuder

11. Which one of the following points is NOT stressed in Ginzberg's theory of occupational choice? 11.___

    A. Compromise   B. Fantasy period
    C. Hierarchy of feelings D. Irreversibility

12. The Division of Vocational Rehabilitation of the State Department of Education is primarily designed to provide which one of the following? 12.___

    A. Vocational training for the physically or mentally handicapped
    B. Vocational training and employment of the school "drop out"
    C. Vocational counseling and placement of children of families receiving public welfare
    D. Vocational placement of youth released from State Training Schools

13. Occupational and labor information prepared and published by the United States Bureau of Labor Statistics is titled 13.___

    A. OCCUPATIONAL INFORMATION FOR COUNSELORS
    B. CAREER OPPORTUNITIES
    C. HANDBOOK OF JOB FACTS
    D. MONTHLY LABOR REVIEW

14. An empirically-keyed inventory designed to measure exclusively interests in non-professional occupations is the 14.___

    A. Kuder Preference Record - Form D, Occupational
    B. Minnesota Vocational Interest Inventory
    C. Brainard Occupational Preference Inventory
    D. Strong Vocational Interest Blank

15. In the ten-year period from 1970 to 1980, the United States labor force increased, on the average, by about how many persons each year?_____ million. 15.____

   A. 1/4   B. $\frac{1}{2}$ C. $1\frac{1}{2}$ D. $2\frac{1}{2}$

16. Unemployment rates vary considerably by occupational group. Which one of the following occupational categories typically registers the LOWEST unemployment rate? 16.____

   A. Laborers
   B. Skilled workers
   C. Sales workers
   D. Professional and technical workers

17. As a result of the post-war baby boom, younger workers have become increasingly important in the labor force. Of the total increase in the labor force, workers under 25 account for about 17.____

   A. three quarters   B. one half
   C. one quarter   D. one tenth

18. The American Counseling Association was founded in 1952 as the 18.____

   A. Community Council
   B. American Personnel and Guidance Association
   C. Vocational Advisory Service
   D. National Vocational Guidance Association

19. The largest numerical occupational category classified as skilled workers by the Census definitions is 19.____

   A. auto mechanics   B. electricians
   C. plumbers   D. carpenters

20. Compared with a high school graduate, recent trends indicate that the school dropout will experience an unemployment rate approximately _____ than graduates. 20.____

   A. fifty percent higher   B. twice as high
   C. three times higher   D. five times higher

21. Of the following, the LARGEST employment category among the professionals is 21.____

   A. accounting   B. engineers
   C. nurses   D. teachers

22. One of the BEST standards for use in evaluating occupational literature has been published by the 22.____

   A. American School Counselor Association
   B. National Manpower Commission
   C. National Vocational Guidance Association
   D. United States Employment Service

23. Employment in the professional, scientific and technical services sector of the economy makes up approximately what percentage of the labor force, according to the Bureau of Labor Statistics?

    A. 2%
    B. 5%
    C. 15%
    D. 20%

24. The MOST economically *disadvantaged* group within the United States is the

    A. American Indian
    B. Mexican-American
    C. Puerto Rican
    D. African-American

25. The MOST detailed descriptions of the activities performed by the worker in an occupation can be found in which of the following?

    A. ENCYCLOPEDIA OF VOCATIONAL GUIDANCE
    B. D.O.T., PART III
    C. MONTHLY LABOR REVIEW
    D. OCCUPATIONAL OUTLOOK HANDBOOK

KEY (CORRECT ANSWERS)

1. D	11. C
2. A	12. A
3. B	13. D
4. C	14. B
5. D	15. C
6. A	16. D
7. C	17. B
8. D	18. B
9. A	19. D
10. D	20. B

21. D
22. C
23. B
24. B
25. D

EXAMINATION SECTION
TEST 1

DIRECTIONS: Each question or incomplete statement is followed by several suggested answers or completions. Select the one that BEST answers the question or completes the statement. *PRINT THE LETTER OF THE CORRECT ANSWER IN THE SPACE AT THE RIGHT.*

1. Which one of the following "suggestions to interviewers" should be AVOIDED? 1.____
    - A. Encourage the client to verbalize his thoughts and feelings.
    - B. Cover as much as possible in each interview.
    - C. Don't hesitate to refer the client to someone else who might be more helpful in the situation.
    - D. The problem which is presented initially, or the one which seems most obvious, often is not the real one.

2. If it seems clear that disturbance in parents' marital relationships is a major factor in causing a child to be emotionally disturbed, the counselor should 2.____
    - A. point this out to the parents and tell them that for the welfare of their children, they should resolve their difficulties
    - B. suggest that he will be willing to discuss their marital difficulties with them
    - C. ignore this and concentrate on helping the child
    - D. tactfully suggest that their marital difficulties may be playing a part in their child's disturbance and offer to refer the parents to a qualified marriage counseling service

3. The process of collecting, analyzing, synthesizing and interpreting information about the client should be 3.____
    - A. completed prior to counseling
    - B. completed early in the counseling process
    - C. limited to counseling which is primarily diagnostic in purpose
    - D. continuous throughout counseling

4. Catharsis, the "emotional unloading" of the client's feelings, has a value in the early stages of counseling because it accomplishes all BUT which one of the following goals? 4.____
    - A. It relieves strong physiological tensions in the client.
    - B. It increases the client's anxiety and therefore his motivation to continue counseling.
    - C. It provides a verbal substitute for "acting out" the client's aggressive feelings.
    - D. It releases emotional energy which the client has been using to maintain his defenses.

5. During the first interview, the counselor can expect the client to participate at his BEST when the counselor 5.____
    - A. structures the nature of the counseling process
    - B. attempts to summarize the client's problem for him
    - C. allows the client to verbalize at his own pace
    - D. tells the client that he understands the presenting problem

6. To obtain the most effective results in change of attitude and behavior through parent education, the leader should be

   A. thoroughly grounded in the whole field of psychology
   B. able to help members of the group look at their own attitudes and behavior in constructive ways
   C. completely confident as to the right solution to problems that may be brought up
   D. a warm, charming, friendly human being

6.____

7. A social worker's report about a client states that a mother has ambivalent feelings concerning her child. This means that the mother

   A. has contradictory emotional reactions concerning her child
   B. is overprotective of the child
   C. strongly rejects the child
   D. is unduly apprehensive about the child's welfare

7.____

8. A psychological report notes, "The client shows little effect." This means that the client

   A. did not take the test too seriously
   B. did not show emotional behavior in situations which normally call for such reactions
   C. did not show signs of fatigue as the testing progressed
   D. reacted to the test situation in a generally favorable manner

8.____

9. A psychologist's report states, in part, that a client exhibits some masochistic symptoms. This will be evident to the counselor through the client's persistent attempts at

   A. self-assertion
   B. self-effacement
   C. inflicting physical harm on others
   D. sexual molestation of others of the same sex

9.____

10. According to research studies, the type of counselor response that is MOST often followed by a client's expression of insight or illumination is

    A. clarification of feeling
    B. reflection of feeling
    C. simple acceptance
    D. exploratory question

10.____

11. Of the following, the BEST way to deal with a 12-year-old boy who feels inferior to his peers is to

    A. provide tasks which he can master with little difficulty
    B. show him how irrational his feelings are
    C. accept his declarations of lack of confidence sympathetically
    D. carefully arrange situations in which he will be obliged to show leadership

11.____

12. In counseling or psychotherapy, the factor which is the MOST important for success tends to be the

    A. counselor's theoretical orientation
    B. counselor's attitudes and feelings toward the client

12.____

C. techniques used by the counselor
D. amount of experience and training possessed by the counselor

13. Transference is an important aspect of

    A. test construction
    B. grade placement
    C. anecdotal record keeping
    D. therapy

14. The MOST desirable way of establishing rapport with a client who comes to the counselor with a problem is to

    A. demonstrate sincere interest in him
    B. offer to do everything possible to solve his problem for him
    C. use the language of the client
    D. promise to keep his problem confidential

15. Role playing has been used as a technique in parent education work. Of the following, the major value is that it

    A. permits parents to express unconscious feelings and thereby solve conflicts
    B. tells a story in a forceful and therefore lasting way
    C. provides an opportunity for the individual to view his problems by standing off and looking at them through the eyes of someone else
    D. brings to light problems people never knew they had

16. If during a counseling situation a client expressed anger about a particular situation, which of the following responses would a non-directive counselor MOST likely make?

    A. "Why are you so angry?"
    B. "Is there any need to get so upset about this?"
    C. "This has really made you very mad, hasn't it?"
    D. "Do you feel better now that you have expressed your anger?"

17. In a counseling process, the counselor should usually give information

    A. whenever it is needed
    B. at the end of the process
    C. in the introductory interview
    D. just before the client would ordinarily request it

18. "After having recognized and clarified feelings and conflicts, it is usually necessary to go beyond the stage of understanding and to elaborate a constructive plan for future action." Which of the following people would NOT go along with the above statement?

    A. Thorne
    B. Robinson
    C. Williamson
    D. Rogers

19. The counselor should focus his attention in the beginning upon

    A. the transference phenomenon
    B. evidences of hostility
    C. the unique characteristics of the particular relationship at hand
    D. indications of client aggressiveness

20. A recent guidance text that stresses the broad developments of our national heritage, our contemporary social setting, our value patterns, and also the integration into guidance of many disciplines-sociology, anthropology, philosophy, psychology-is

   A. FOUNDATIONS OF GUIDANCE - Miller
   B. GUIDANCE POLICY AND PRACTICE - Mathewson
   C. GUIDANCE IN TODAY'S SCHOOLS - Mortenson & Schmuller
   D. GUIDANCE SERVICES - Humphreys, Traxler & North

21. Which one of the following characteristics of counseling is inconsistent with the others?

   A. Counseling is more than advice-giving.
   B. Counseling involves something more than the solution to an immediate problem.
   C. Counseling concerns itself with attitudes rather than actions.
   D. Counseling involves intellectual rather than emotional attitudes as its basic raw material.

22. One approach to counseling has been labeled "non-directive". The word "non-directive" derives from the fact that, in this approach to counseling, the counselor

   A. does not tell the client what he should do
   B. makes the client responsible for the direction of the course of the interviews
   C. does not make judgments about the behavior of the client
   D. avoids possible areas of threat to the client

23. Of the following personality traits, which would be LEAST essential for an effective counselor to possess?

   A. Extroversion   B. Objectivity
   C. Security   D. Sensitivity

24. Interpretation as a therapeutic tool is considered a hindrance to therapy progress by

   A. orthodox Freudians   B. neo-analysts
   C. Rogerians   D. Adlerians

25. The current interpersonal behavior of the client is probably MOST important as a therapy topic to which two analytic theorists?

   A. Freud and Adler   B. Adler and Rank
   C. Freud and Rank   D. Horney and Sullivan

KEY (CORRECT ANSWERS)

1. B
2. D
3. D
4. B
5. C

6. B
7. A
8. B
9. B
10. C

11. A
12. B
13. D
14. A
15. C

16. C
17. A
18. D
19. C
20. A

21. D
22. B
23. A
24. C
25. D

TEST 2

DIRECTIONS: Each question or incomplete statement is followed by several suggested answers or completions. Select the one that BEST answers the question or completes the statement. *PRINT THE LETTER OF THE CORRECT ANSWER IN THE SPACE AT THE RIGHT.*

1. When a counselor is listening to a client, it is MOST important that he be able to

    A. show interest and agreement with what the client is saying
    B. paraphrase what the client is saying
    C. understand the significance of what the client is saying
    D. differentiate between fact and fiction in what the client is saying

2. On which one of the following is successful counseling LEAST likely to depend?

    A. The counselor's theoretical orientation
    B. The counselor's ability to bring the client's feelings and attitudes into the open
    C. The counselor's diagnostic ability
    D. The client's readiness for counseling

3. A client is referred to you for counseling against his will and is suspicious and uncooperative. You should

    A. explain to him that you cannot help him unless he is prepared to cooperate
    B. explain that you are not taking sides and that you will be impartial
    C. show him that you know how he feels and encourage him to talk about it
    D. explain that you are on his side and will listen sympathetically to anything that he might care to bring up

4. Which one of the following would NOT be considered a basic objective of the first interview between a client and a counselor?

    A. Beginning a sound counseling relationship
    B. Identifying the client's real problem
    C. Opening up the area of client feelings and attitudes
    D. Clarifying the nature of the counseling process for the client

5. All of the following counselor statements or actions are appropriate techniques for ending an interview EXCEPT

    A. "Our time is nearly up. Is there something else you have in mind for today?"
    B. "Let's see now. Suppose we go over what we've accomplished today."
    C. Counselor may glance at his watch and say, "When would you like to come in again?"
    D. Counselor may shuffle papers on desk and say, "Now, let's see; when is my next appointment?"

6. It has been recognized in recent literature that the value structure of the individual counselor has what kind of effect on the counseling process?

    A. Direct   B. Indirect
    C. Little   D. None

7. The intensive study of the same individuals over a fairly long period of time represents the

   A. cross-sectional approach
   B. longitudinal approach
   C. clinical approach
   D. biographical approach

8. Of the following techniques, the one which is MOST characteristic of non-directive or client-centered therapy is

   A. encouraging transference
   B. free association
   C. reflection of feeling
   D. permissive questioning

9. In making predictions about how a client will behave in a given situation, a counselor

   A. should limit himself to those situations for which "actuarial" data are available
   B. must rely on "clinical" judgment in many situations but use "actuarial" data wherever possible
   C. should rely on "clinical" judgment in all situations, since they are more valid than "actuarial" predictions
   D. always uses "actuarial" data, but modifies them in light of his "clinical" impression of the client

10. A research study that establishes an hypothesis, sets up control groups, collects data, and generalizes from the data is

    A. formulative
    B. diagnostic
    C. experimental
    D. exploratory

11. The MOST usable single index of the social and economic status of all the members of any family is

    A. occupation of the father
    B. religious affiliation of the family
    C. location of the home in the community
    D. socio-economic rating by neighbors

12. When a counselor does NOT understand the meaning of a response that a counselee has made, the counselor usually should

    A. proceed to another topic
    B. admit his lack of understanding and ask for clarification
    C. act as if he understands so that the counselee's confidence in him is not shaken
    D. ask the counselee to choose his words more carefully

13. When the counselor makes a response which touches off a high degree of resistance in the counselee, he should

    A. apologize and rephrase his remark in a less threatening manner
    B. accept the resistance
    C. ignore the counselee's resistance
    D. recognize that little more will be accomplished in the interview and offer another appointment

14. Directive and non-directive counseling are two emphases in counseling theory and practice. From the pairs of names listed below, indicate the two that are representative of the Directive school.

    A. Thorne and Williamson
    B. Rogers and Thorne
    C. Williamson and Sullivan
    D. Sullivan and Rogers

15. Rogerian counseling theory is based on the assumption that the potential and tendency for growth toward a fully functioning personality is present in

    A. a few "self-actualized" persons
    B. most people of above average intelligence
    C. people whose behavior can be considered as "normal" and socially effective
    D. all people

16. Anecdotal records should contain which type(s) of information?

    A. Evaluations
    B. Interpretations
    C. Factual reports
    D. Prognoses

17. RESISTANCE in relation to psychological counseling typically refers to the

    A. client's defenses against his inner conflicts
    B. counselor's unwillingness to deal with the client's emotional problems
    C. client's having enough ego strength so that he can face his problems
    D. counselor's having enough ego strength so that he can help the client face his problems

18. On which one of the following does the democratic leader specifically rely? His ability to

    A. listen and tactfully guide the discussion in the direction he has planned and the members' willingness to cooperate
    B. diagnose situations, to interpret and explain them to the members and their willingness to accept
    C. discern the issues which the members could profitably discuss and his willingness to allow them with his help to do so
    D. understand the meaning of the response from the member's frame of reference and his willingness for them to make decisions

19. Advisement in counseling is MOST effective when the counselee is in a state of

    A. perceiving his problem as related to a conflict with inner forces
    B. minimal conflict and of optimal readiness for action
    C. perceiving his problem as related to an external conflict
    D. feeling extremely ambivalent about his self-concept

20. Of the following, the MOST valid use of projective techniques is the study of the

    A. problems which an individual faces
    B. cultural effects upon an individual
    C. inner world of an individual
    D. human relationships of an individual

21. Diagnosis is NOT regarded as a helpful antecedent to counseling by   21._____

    A. Cottle   B. Rogers
    C. Thorne   D. Williamson

22. The beginning counselor must be alert to interferences to rapport. Which one of the following is NOT considered an intereference?   22._____

    A. Injecting the counselor's present mood
    B. Engaging in "small talk" at the start of the interview
    C. Registering surprise or dismay
    D. Emphasizing the counselor's ability

23. There is some evidence according to Rogers that counseling is more effective with   23._____

    A. younger adults or higher intelligence
    B. older adults of higher intelligence
    C. younger adults of lower intelligence
    D. older adults of lower intelligence

24. In assisting with the scheduling of interviews for educational planning, the counselor should suggest that group instruction   24._____

    A. follow the counseling interview
    B. is not necessary when individual interviews can be scheduled since each case is different
    C. precede the counseling
    D. may either precede or follow the counseling interview

25. A client has requested an interview with the counselor to discuss a personal problem. In general, the BEST way to begin the interview is to   25._____

    A. come directly to the point and encourage the client to talk about his problem
    B. assure him that everything discussed will be confidential
    C. offer to help him in every way possible
    D. inquire whether he has discussed the problem with anyone else

KEY (CORRECT ANSWERS)

1. C
2. A
3. C
4. B
5. D

6. A
7. B
8. C
9. B
10. C

11. A
12. B
13. B
14. A
15. D

16. C
17. A
18. C
19. B
20. C

21. B
22. B
23. A
24. C
25. A

EXAMINATION SECTION
TEST 1

DIRECTIONS: Each question or incomplete statement is followed by several suggested answers or completions. Select the one that BEST answers the question or completes the statement. *PRINT THE LETTER OF THE CORRECT ANSWER IN THE SPACE AT THE RIGHT.*

1. When a counselee describes a problem which is similar to one the counselor has had, the counselor usually should

    A. tell the counselee how he reacted in similar circumstances
    B. suggest solutions which worked for him
    C. describe his own experiences, but disguise them by saying they happened to another of his counselees
    D. make no reference to his experience

    1.____

2. Of the following, the MOST highly specialized process in guidance is

    A. testing
    B. occupational study
    C. interviewing
    D. counseling

    2.____

3. Which of the following is the MOST fundamental aim of guidance?

    A. Solve client's problems
    B. Counsel clients concerning problems
    C. Develop self-direction
    D. Direct the client to strive for excellence

    3.____

4. A counselor forecasts the extent to which the counselee may or may not make a desirable or satisfying adaptation to his situation. Williamson referred to this step in the counseling process as

    A. synthesis
    B. prognosis
    C. follow-up
    D. diagnosis

    4.____

5. A fundamental assumption made by the client-centered school of counseling is that

    A. diagnosis is essential to effective counseling
    B. every individual possesses a "tendency toward growth"
    C. responsibility for client actions is assumed by the counselor
    D. the counselor's role is primarily one of giving information to the counselee

    5.____

6. Referral of a client to other agencies should be made

    A. after a long period of counseling has proved ineffectual
    B. only with the client's and his parent's consent
    C. as soon as the needed adjustment lies outside of client's, as well as counselor's, control
    D. after consultation with teachers and administration

    6.____

7. According to field theory, individuals who are initially faced with a problem tend to seek

   A. long involved indirect solutions
   B. simple direct solutions
   C. outside help in forcing a solution
   D. means of withdrawing from the problem

8. In regard to client activity, the goal of counseling agreed upon by all methodologies is

   A. integrated controlled behavior
   B. release of feeling and negative emotion
   C. more individuals who understand themselves
   D. conformity to the cultural mores

9. A counselor who is primarily concerned with analyzing and diagnosing a client's problems, collecting and synthesizing data about the client, and making predictions about the consequences of various client decisions would BEST be classified as using which method of counseling? The

   A. *clinical* method as described by Williamson
   B. *client-centered* method as described by Rogers
   C. *communications* method as described by Robinson
   D. *learning* method as described by Dollard & Miller

10. Most definitions would NOT include which of the following as a necessary aspect of counseling?

    A. The counselor and client meet face-to-face.
    B. The client is experiencing a degree of emotional disturbance.
    C. A unique learning opportunity is provided for the client.
    D. The counselor brings special competence to the counseling relationship.

11. The *initial* counseling interview is considered by many to be hardest.
    Which one of the following is NOT an essential objective of this session? To

    A. develop a sound working relationship with the individual
    B. make a diagnosis of the client's problem
    C. orient the client to the nature of the counseling process
    D. provide an atmosphere that allows the individual to express freely his attitudes and feelings

12. A powerful dynamic in the counseling process and usually the very antithesis of its counterpart in the instructional process is

    A. encouraging accuracy
    B. emphasizing structure
    C. encouraging sequential orderly thinking
    D. processing ambiguity

13. Counseling techniques are useful in working with advantaged, bright or creative children. Fundamental is a counseling atmosphere that is

    A. non-threatening
    B. urging for creativity
    C. highly charged to stimulate excitement
    D. pretty well structured

14. Which one of the following counseling approaches emphasizes differential diagnosis in the treatment of individual clients?

    A. Trait- and factor-centered
    B. Self-theory
    C. Communications
    D. Psychoanalytic

15. The school of counseling theory, characterized by the attempt to observe behavior from the point of view of the individual himself (i.e., his own frame of reference), is known as

    A. organismic
    B. neo-Freudianism
    C. existentialism
    D. phenomenology

16. Of the following, which characteristic do counseling theorists consider MOST essential to the effectiveness of a counselor?

    A. Extroversion
    B. Persuasiveness
    C. Serenity
    D. Objectivity

17. The counseling approach which uses any of a variety of techniques which BEST suit individual situations is called

    A. instinctive
    B. specific
    C. conditioning
    D. eclectic

18. Mental testing, statistics, and measurement are identified *most closely* with which one of the following counseling approaches?

    A. Neobehavioral
    B. Trait- and factor-centered
    C. Psychoanalytic
    D. Communications

19. The "self-actualization" process is the central tendency of which one of the following approaches in counseling?

    A. Neobehavioral
    B. Communications
    C. Self-theory
    D. Psychoanalytic

20. In counseling, the LEAST acceptable introduction in phrasing an interpretative statement is which one of the following?

    A. "It seems as though..."
    B. "Do you suppose that..."
    C. "It probably would be better if..."
    D. "I'm wondering if..."

21. The term "ambiguity" in counseling refers to the degree of, openness or uncertainty that exists in the minds of both counselor and client regarding what is supposed to happen next.
    The ULTIMATE degree of ambiguity in counseling is represented by the use of

    A. open-ended leads
    B. depth interpretation
    C. "yes" and "no" questions
    D. free association

22. The client says, "I can't seem to get along with the other kids."
    Of the following, the MOST appropriate counselor response is:

    A. "Have you done your part?"
    B. "Let's talk about it."
    C. "You're too reserved and too cold."
    D. "You don't care very much about it."

23. In psychoanalytically-oriented counseling, the responsibility for the client's bringing up and talking about important material lies

    A. *exclusively* with the client
    B. *primarily* with the client, with the help of the counselor
    C. *primarily* with the counselor, with the cooperation of the client
    D. *exclusively* with the counselor

24. Research shows that, regardless of theoretical persuasion, experienced counselors as compared with less experienced counselors tend to

    A. use a wider range of techniques
    B. rely primarily on reflection of feeling
    C. use deeper interpretations
    D. take more responsibility for content

25. STRUCTURING in counseling is the process of

    A. building rapport in the initial interview
    B. establishing the ground rules for the counselor
    C. determining the client's real problem
    D. communicating and sharing expectations about counseling

KEY (CORRECT ANSWERS)

1. D
2. D
3. C
4. B
5. B

6. C
7. B
8. A
9. A
10. B

11. B
12. D
13. A
14. A
15. D

16. D
17. D
18. B
19. C
20. C

21. D
22. B
23. B
24. A
25. D

TEST 2

DIRECTIONS: Each question or incomplete statement is followed by several suggested answers or completions. Select the one that BEST answers the question or completes the statement. *PRINT THE LETTER OF THE CORRECT ANSWER IN THE SPACE AT THE RIGHT.*

1. Of non-white youngsters in the United States who drop out before completing 4 years of high school, what proportion come from families earning less than $20,000?

    A. 25% B. 40% C. Over 50% D. Over 90%

2. Educational attainment has been rising. Median school years of attainment for persons now holding clerical or sales jobs average

    A. more than 12 years B. less than 12 years
    C. more than 10 years D. less than 10 years

3. From the client-centered point of view of counseling, information about the client's skills, personality, etc. are best used

    A. to help the counselor to understand the client better
    B. to help the client to understand himself better
    C. as a basis for the counselor's suggestions, which the client is free to reject
    D. as a part of the counselor's diagnosis in deciding how best to work with the client

4. Appropriate responses for a counselor include all of the following EXCEPT

    A. "If I were you..."
    B. "Can you tell me more about...?"
    C. "How do you feel about...?"
    D. "How long has this been going on...?"

5. During the early stages of a counseling relationship, a client engages in long periods of silence and appears to have difficulty in discussing questions which the counselor raises. A psychoanalytically-oriented counselor would *probably* interpret these silences and difficulties as signs of

    A. lack of rapport
    B. frustrated oral needs
    C. the client's inability to analyze his problems
    D. resistance to dealing with emotional problems

6. The single recent book which focuses specifically on problems of professionalization in counseling in the present society and makes dramatic recommendations for counselor training is THE COUNSELOR IN A CHANGING WORLD. The author is

    A. Dugald S. Arbuckle B. Edward C. Glanz
    C. Leslie E. Moser D. C. Gilbert Wrenn

7. All of above the following are identified with existential counseling EXCEPT

    A. Frankl B. May
    C. Van Kamm D. Eysenck

8. In the final analysis, realization of potential by the individual depends upon

   A. his abilities
   B. the limits imposed by his society and culture
   C. subjective interactional factors
   D. all of the above

9. Which one of the following is the MOST important deterrent to evaluation of guidance programs? Lack of

   A. objective data
   B. suitable criteria
   C. research skills among guidance workers
   D. data processing equipment

10. Acculturation, the process of acquiring values different from those of the culture into which one is born, can BEST be promoted through guidance of

    A. introducing the student to the new culture
    B. showing the student how the culture into which he was born is inadequate
    C. supporting the individual in learning the new culture and by rewarding him for the new learning
    D. showing the student that cultural differences are relatively unimportant

11. The client speaks so low that you cannot hear what he is saying.
    The BEST technique to use in handling this would be to

    A. confront the client with the problem
    B. pretend that you can hear him
    C. respond in like manner
    D. interpret this action to him as an "interpersonal defense mechanism"

12. All of the following are important in the "social-psychological" theories of counseling EXCEPT

    A. life style
    B. cognitive processes
    C. interpersonal relationships
    D. need for identity

13. In distinguishing between counseling and clinical psychology, which of the following tends to be TRUE of the counselor but not of the clinician?

    A. The major focus is on the normal, adaptive resources of the client's personality
    B. The use of psychological test data to contribute to a better understanding of the client
    C. A supportive and accepting relationship is developed
    D. The disintegrative, disturbed aspects of the client's personality receive major attention

14. Which of the following words is MOST similar in meaning to "reliability"?

    A. Consistency   B. Interpretability
    C. Objectivity   D. Truthfulness

15. Which of the following can be classified as an observational device?

    A. Anecdotal records
    B. Interest inventories
    C. Projective technique
    D. Personality inventories

16. As a guidance counselor, you may often be consulted by parents about how to respond more helpfully to teenagers. Which one of the following judgments about parent-teenager relationships is false?

    A. Parents' approval of work well done and pride in accomplishment means a great deal to the teenager, even though he brushes it off.
    B. For the sake of the young person's self-respect, it is a good idea to criticize him as much as possible.
    C. Giving a teenager opportunity for being in with a group is closely related to school progress.
    D. Parents' recognition and appreciation of good school progress, without putting on heavy pressure, is a help in keeping it up

17. In counseling, the term "understanding" refers to

    A. the counselor's ability to communicate how a client's behavior appears to other people
    B. the counselor's skill in grasping meanings the client's comments convey
    C. the counselor's adeptness in anticipating feelings of the client
    D. the counselor's knowledge of dynamics of personality

18. Of the following, the MOST significant difference between "psychotherapy" and "counseling" is in the

    A. goals and expected outcomes
    B. techniques used
    C. amount of psychological insight involved
    D. professional background of the counselor

19. Appropriate "bridges" for the counselor in counseling are all of the following EXCEPT

    A. "Let's move on to..."
    B. "We were talking about..."
    C. "What was it you said about...?"
    D. "How does this fit in with what you said earlier?"

20. From the client-centered point of view, "understanding" in counseling is BEST thought of as

    A. diagnosing the client's motivational structure
    B. seeing the client's world as he sees it
    C. following and accepting the client's spoken words
    D. the ability to predict future actions

21. The statement of a client MOST indicative of *transference* feelings is:

    A. "I really didn't feel like coming here today."
    B. "My mother doesn't approve of my talking to you."
    C. "If only you would tell me what I should do."
    D. "You remind me of my father."

22. In counseling, "reflection" refers to

    A. a restatement of the counselee's comment
    B. clarification of the content of the remark
    C. the counselor's perception of the feelings being expressed
    D. a non-committal statement such as "uh huh"

23. In the given paradigm, all are CORRECTLY matched EXCEPT:

	Counseling Model	Predominant Goal
A.	Psychoanalytic	insight
B.	Teacher-learner	sound decision and self-understanding
C.	Behavioral	shaping of specific responses
D.	Client-centered	catharsis

24. Freud believes that the client builds defenses against his inner conflicts when the therapeutic process tempts him to express conflictual impulses. These defenses result in resistance.
    According to Freud, such resistance in successful counseling

    A. is unavoidable
    B. is carefully avoided by the counselor
    C. indicates the counselor has proceeded too fast
    D. does not occur

25. Existential counseling includes all of the following characteristics EXCEPT

    A. a belief in universal values
    B. a subjective view of reality
    C. the total empathic response of the therapist
    D. the individual's intense awareness of his contingency and his freedom

KEY (CORRECT ANSWERS)

1. C
2. A
3. B
4. A
5. D

6. D
7. D
8. D
9. B
10. C

11. A
12. B
13. A
14. A
15. A

16. B
17. B
18. A
19. A
20. B

21. D
22. C
23. D
24. A
25. A

EXAMINATION SECTION
TEST 1

DIRECTIONS: Each question or incomplete statement is followed by several suggested answers or completions. Select the one that BEST answers the question or completes the statement. *PRINT THE LETTER OF THE CORRECT ANSWER IN THE SPACE AT THE RIGHT.*

1. Counselors adhering to the personality theory espoused by C.G. Jung often have to help people with problems related to what Jung called *individuation*.
   Jung defined this term as the process

   A. which occurs when adolescents leave home to establish their own residences
   B. occurring throughout life in which a person is becoming an individual
   C. through which parents come to have unique patterns of interaction with each of their children
   D. which is an outgrowth of the psychoanalytic principle of determinism

   1.____

2. A counselor completing a report for an insurance company was required to indicate whether a client had a phobia or an anxiety reaction.
   The counselor was able to indicate the correct classification because the counselor knew that the PRIMARY distinction between the two conditions is the

   A. age of onset of severe psychological distress
   B. ease with which the symptoms are eliminated
   C. frequency of symptom occurrence
   D. specificity of the fear-causing source

   2.____

3. Erikson presented an eight-stage theory of human development, the last stage of which he entitled Integrity versus Despair. A person's challenge in this stage is to achieve acceptance of the finality of life.
   Erikson postulated that such acceptance could be achieved *only* if the person had

   A. reached a parallel level of moral development
   B. established an economic environment such that the person need not be concerned about having good living conditions
   C. successfully met the challenges of the previous stages
   D. developed the ability to distinguish among the various roles the individual had filled in life

   3.____

4. Humanists in the existential tradition assert that personal decisions are (personally) effective only if they are made consistent with personal beliefs and principles, and regardless of whether they are in agreement with those of most people or the known consequences of the decisions.
   This assertion also is an appropriate description of which of Kohlberg's stages of moral development?

   A. Naively egotistic orientation
   B. Respect for authority and social order
   C. Contractual-legalistic orientation
   D. Conscience orientation

   4.____

5. A counselor was hired to develop educational activities that would promote development of gender-fair (i.e., non sex-role stereotypic) attitudes among older elementary-school-age children. The counselor decided to develop the activities within the context of social learning theory.
   Which of the following activities would be MOST appropriate for use by the counselor?

   A. Having the children view movies that depict males in so-called traditionally feminine occupations (e.g., nursing) or activities (e.g., ironing) and vice versa
   B. Providing some reward (e.g., a small candy) to children who make gender-fair statements during a discussion of *what people do when they grow up*
   C. Instructing the children to ask their parents what their parents' beliefs are about appropriate roles for women and men
   D. Having the children share what they believe are each of their parent's feelings about activities they do (e.g., active and passive play behaviors)

6. In attempting to understand the life perspectives and characteristics of their clients, some counselors use Kohlberg's theory of moral development as a theoretical framework. These counselors know that Kohlberg's theory includes three progressive levels culminating in

   A. self-actualization, wherein the individual is fully humanistic
   B. principled thought, wherein the individual adopts a self-accepted set of standards of behavior
   C. androgyny, wherein the individual exhibits both male and female stereotypic behaviors
   D. personhood, wherein the individual is free from moral dilemmas

7. A professional counselor determines fees for monthly consultation services on a job-by-job basis.
   This is an example of which of the following types of reinforcement schedules?

   A. Variable interval   B. Fixed interval
   C. Variable ratio   D. Fixed ratio

8. Competitiveness between children in the same family is known as

   A. sibling rivalry   B. the Oedipus conflict
   C. the Electra conflict   D. the Foundling conflict

9. A counselor in a social services agency working with economically deprived immigrants would focus on the person's most urgent need.
   The FIRST priority would be the need for

   A. love   B. shelter and food
   C. friendship   D. education

10. The BEST descriptor of the emotion that results when a feeling of fear is not understood by the person experiencing it is

    A. anxiety   B. affect   C. anger   D. arousal

11. Many members of the counseling profession have engaged in social reform efforts intended to reduce spouse abuse.
    These efforts have had limited effect because

    A. spouse abuse occurs primarily among persons of low socioeconomic status, a group of people not generally prone to seek counseling services
    B. many people, both males and females, believe that spouse abuse is a *family matter* and, therefore, not subject to intervention from persons outside the family
    C. increasing incidence of incarceration of spouse abusers has reduced the need for counseling services
    D. all of the above

11.____

12. A counselor was working with a client who had been referred by a supervisor because the client had been having problems with co-workers, problems primarily attributable to the client's prejudicial attitudes toward ethnic minorities. The counselor asked how the client had come to hold the (prejudicial) attitudes the client was presenting. The client replied, *I don't really know or care. It just makes those folks easier to understand.*
    The client's statements reflect which of the following models that have been used to explain the formation of prejudicial attitudes?

    A. Social learning   B. Information processing
    C. Social conflict   D. Authoritarianism

12.____

13. A client was referred to a counselor by a physician. On the physician's advice, the client had been taking valium to alleviate *minor instances of stress.*
    Initially, small doses of valium were sufficient to alleviate the client's stress. However, over a period of approximately one year, the client had found it necessary to take increasingly larger doses to bring about similar stress reduction.
    The counselor surmised that the client had developed a(n) _____ reaction to the valium.

    A. psychological dependence
    B. addiction
    C. physical dependence
    D. tolerance

13.____

14. Because of the nature of the counseling process, some concepts from the field of speech and communications are readily applied to counseling. For example, counselors often find it appropriate to give (i.e., send) persuasive messages to clients. Such messages are more likely to be received (i.e., heard and accepted) if the counselor, as the message sender, exhibits certain characteristics.
    Which of the following is NOT a primary characteristic of effective persuasive communicators?

    A. Emotionality   B. Attractiveness
    C. Expertness   D. Trustworthiness

14.____

15. In recent years, the language used in federal and many state legislative acts relative to counseling services for persons with handicaps has tended to shift from the use of general categorical definitions to noncategorical definitions of functional limitations of handicapping conditions.
    This change appears to reflect a realization that

15.____

A. the medical (i.e., physical) diagnosis is the most accurate basis for determining an appropriate level of funding
B. a specific disability has essentially the same effect in any educational or work setting
C. funding bases should not incorporate considerations of categories of disabilities
D. all categorically disabled people do not have the same functional limitations in all work or education situations

16. Research on the development in a person of a so-called *humanistic life outlook* has shown that it is facilitated by

    A. formal educational experiences
    B. observational learning experiences
    C. diverse interpersonal interactions
    D. all of the above

17. When persons who are characteristically shy and withdrawn participate in *assertiveness training*, initially they experience uncertainty and self-doubt. Counselors refer to this social-psychological concept as

    A. cognitive dissonance   B. dissociation
    C. individuation   D. acculturation

18. A group of people living together with prescribed patterns of interdependent behavior could be BEST described as a

    A. culture   B. society   C. class   D. cult

19. Which of the following does NOT influence conformity to the expected standards of behavior within a culture?

    A. Physical punishment   B. Praise
    C. Acceptance   D. Events

20. In counseling older adults to achieve greater life satisfaction, counseling goals are more easily defined with the recognition that life satisfaction among older persons is PRIMARILY related to

    A. economic well-being   B. sexuality
    C. self-concept   D. all of the above

21. A counselor who follows an eclectic approach to counseling PRIMARILY bases the choice of utilized techniques upon

    A. the severity of the emotional distress exhibited by the client
    B. the client's intellectual, emotional, and environmental resources
    C. whether the client was referred or volunteered for counseling
    D. the theoretical orientation espoused in the counselor's professional preparation program

22. Client: *I just can't see myself working in a hospital, being around sick kids all day.*
    Counselor: *You just don't like kids.*
    The counselor in this example has made which of the following types of reflection error?

    A. Depth   B. Capitulation
    C. Meaning   D. Syntax

23. The counseling technique used by the counselor to explain to a client the logical Inconsistencies in the client's statements is known as

    A. confrontation
    B. summarization
    C. paradoxical intention
    D. systematic desensitization

24. In the context of the reality therapy approach to counseling, the counselor strives to achieve a counseling relationship in which the counselor assumes a(n) _____ role in decision making relative to the client.

    A. superordinate
    B. equal
    C. subordinate
    D. antithetical

25. In Schein's *Doctor-Patient* model of consultation, which of the following conditions must be met for the consultation process to be effective?

    A. The consultee correctly interprets the symptoms identified.
    B. The consultee trusts that the consultant has provided accurate diagnostic information.
    C. The consultee is willing to implement the suggestions made by the consultant.
    D. All of the above conditions must be met.

26. A client comes to a counselor complaining of *being generally unhappy*. However, the client is unable to clarify further the nature of the unhappiness other than through vague allusions to being not interested in anything.
    At this point in the process, the counselor would be BEST advised to

    A. confront the client's inability to clarify the reasons for the unhappiness
    B. explore activities that the client enjoyed in the past
    C. use active-listening skills until the client is better able to describe the problem
    D. generate and discuss possible reasons for the client's unhappiness

27. Client: *Most of the time things are fine, but I hate it when my parents fight. It makes me want to run away from home.*
    Counselor: *Is it possible that you both love and hate your parents?*
    The counselor's response is an example of the counseling skill known as

    A. reflection
    B. interpretation
    C. summarization
    D. confrontation

28. Which of the following is a basic assumption underlying effective use of Caplan's Mental Health Consultation model?

    A. Mental health consultation is a supplement to other problem-solving mechanisms within an organization.
    B. Consultee attitudes and affect must be dealth with directly in the mental health consultation process.
    C. The technical expertise of the mental health consultant is sufficient for design of an effective intervention.
    D. The consultant and consultee share responsibility for case management.

29. Ellis' Rational Emotive Therapy and Meichenbaum's Cognitive Behavior Modification approaches to counseling are similar in that both hold that

    A. a client's cognitions are *hypotheses to be tested,* not absolute facts or truths
    B. clients should perform *personal experiments* to determine if cognitions and beliefs are consistent with objective reality
    C. *restructuring of cognitions* is an important aspect of therapeutic change
    D. all of the above

30. Clients and counselors sit closer together, presumably reflecting being psychologically closer, when they are similar in terms of factors such as age, social status, and general appearance (e.g., style of clothing worn).
    However, research in proxemics also has shown that forward (upper body) trunk lean by a counselor is likely to cause a negative, distancing reaction initially in a client who is

    A. depressed and crying
    B. less intelligent than the counselor
    C. a different race from the counselor
    D. much shorter than the counselor

31. Although group effectiveness is difficult to define and is related to the purposes and leadership of the group, some general principles have been agreed upon. For example, group processes generally are most effective when the group

    A. has an authoritarian leader who maintains interpersonal rules and directions for the group
    B. develops new ways of functioning in response to emerging needs and patterns of interaction among group members
    C. identifies group members who inhibit movement toward the group's goals
    D. works on several group tasks simultaneously, thereby increasing group efficiency

32. A counseling group member stated, *I feel so much better knowing that many of you have had similar problems. I guess we're all in the same boat!*
    This member's statement is an example of a group process phenomenon known as

    A. transference   B. universality
    C. catharsis   D. intellectualization

33. In some counseling groups the members feel dependent upon the group counselor (leader) for direction and movement and are passive in other ways as well, and the group counselor is easily fatigued and irritated because of the responsibility to *make everything work* in the group.
    According to Yalom (among others), this situation is MOST likely to arise in groups

    A. that have failed to establish self-disclosure as an appropriate behavior for group members
    B. in which unstructured, freely interactive behavior is the norm for group members
    C. in which the meaningfulness of the group to each of the respective members is too high
    D. that have not assumed responsibility for their own functioning

34. Which of the following is the LEAST important consideration that a group leader should employ in the selection of potentially appropriate strategies to be used in the group?

    A. The types of people who will constitute the group
    B. The leader's self-knowledge
    C. The members' previous experience in groups
    D. The extent to which the leader will be involved in the group

35. The members of a group seemed to be rebelling against the group counselor's leadership, *fighting* with one another to establish dominance in the group, confronting the group counselor as well as one another, and generally being in a state of conflict.
    Based on these characteristics and behaviors, the group counselor determined that the group was in which of the following stages of group development?

    A. Orientation   B. Transition
    C. Action   D. Completion

36. Counselors know that groups are formed for different purposes. For example, in some groups the primary goal is to yield some specified outcome, or *product,* while in others the primary goal is to focus on the *process* of interaction within the group.
    Which one of the following types of groups is more product than process oriented?

    A. Behavioral   B. Transactional-analysis
    C. Adlerian   D. Client-centered

37. In the context of group counseling, members who are high in conformity also tend to be high in

    A. independence   B. authoritarianism
    C. intelligence   D. superiority

38. Counselors refer to the study of *person-to-person relationships* within a group situation as

    A. syntaxicality   B. homeostatis
    C. sociometry   D. psychodrama

39. Which of the following is NOT a goal of Gestalt counseling groups?

    A. Helping individuals achieve integration
    B. Helping group members *grow up*
    C. Helping individuals accept anxiety as a part of life
    D. All of the above are Gestalt counseling goals

40. A specific technique for reinforcing desirable behaviors by pairing them with incompatible behaviors and incorporating principles of relaxation is

    A. satiation
    B. extinction gradient delineation
    C. mediation maximization
    D. systematic desensitization

KEY (CORRECT ANSWERS)

1. B	11. B	21. B	31. B
2. D	12. B	22. C	32. B
3. C	13. D	23. A	33. D
4. D	14. A	24. B	34. C
5. A	15. D	25. D	35. B
6. B	16. D	26. C	36. A
7. C	17. A	27. C	37. B
8. A	18. B	28. A	38. C
9. B	19. D	29. D	39. D
10. A	20. D	30. C	40. D

TEST 2

DIRECTIONS: Each question or incomplete statement is followed by several suggested answers or completions. Select the one that BEST answers the question or completes the statement. *PRINT THE LETTER OF THE CORRECT ANSWER IN THE SPACE AT THE RIGHT.*

1. At the conclusion of a year-long career counseling activity designed specifically for 34 *underemployed* persons, you are able to report to your supervisors that 22 of the participants changed to *training/education appropriate jobs*, 4 became unemployed, 5 remained in their same jobs, and 3 dropped out of the counseling program.
   This information is which of the following types of evaluation data?

   A. Process   B. Context   C. Product   D. Validity

   1._____

2. The *compensatory* theory of leisure suggests that a certified public accountant would enjoy _____, whereas the *spill-over* theory of leisure suggests that the accountant would enjoy _____ as a leisure activity.

   A. racquetball; chess
   B. backgammon; computerized games
   C. golf; tennis
   D. reading mysteries; bowling

   2._____

3. A counselor who works with adolescents is familiar with the knowledge that they tend to overselect professional positions and occupations when asked about *what they are planning to do for a living when they grow up*.
   In terms of Gelatt's decision-making paradigm, adolescents tend to have errors in their _____ systems.

   A. value   B. prediction
   C. generalization   D. decision

   3._____

4. A counselor who is following Super's theory of career development would not be surprised to learn that a person whom the counselor believed to be in the *Establishment* stage had

   A. quit work (altogether)
   B. changed jobs
   C. sought preretirement counseling
   D. been promoted to a management position

   4._____

5. One of the PRIMARY differences in clients' uses of career counseling resources in print media format (e.g., DICTIONARY OF OCCUPATIONAL TITLES or OCCUPATIONAL OUTLOOK HANDBOOK) and those in computerized format (e.g., CHOICES, DISCOVER II, SIGI, or ECES) is the

   A. number of jobs/occupations for which information is available
   B. speed with which information can be retrieved for use
   C. lack of need for counselors when the computerized format is used
   D. lack of need for the computerized format when the print media format is used

   5._____

6. A counselor who structures a career counseling group to help group members understand a *fields and levels* approach to careers is following the theory of

   A. Super B. Roe C. Holland D. Tiedeman

7. The concept of *career maturity* has been described and researched MOST extensively by

   A. Crites B. Hoyt C. Tiedeman D. Ginzberg

8. Which of the following is NOT one of the four major elements in Super's approach to career development?

   A. Vocational maturity
   B. Career patterns
   C. Values clarification
   D. Vocational life stages

9. The DICTIONARY OF OCCUPATIONAL TITLES

   A. would not be useful in face-to-face counseling with an individual
   B. is more useful than the OCCUPATIONAL OUTLOOK HANDBOOK
   C. could be useful in helping a counselee expand occupational options
   D. would be useful at the conclusion of the counseling process

10. Career counseling should include

    A. exploration of values and attitudes
    B. information and factual data about counselees, resources
    C. recognition of counselees' needs, conflicts, and relationships
    D. all of the above

11. A student obtained a score of 93 on a test having a standard error of measurement of 4 points.
    In interpreting the results, the counselor correctly informed the student that

    A. the student could not get a score above ninety-seven no matter how many times the test was retaken by the student
    B. the student had scored among the top eleven percent of those who had taken the test
    C. the student had achieved a score that was at least four points above the national mean
    D. more than likely the student would get a score between eighty-nine and ninety-seven if the student took the test again

12. In a consulting capacity with a local business college, a counselor had recommended administration of a clerical aptitude test to students in each of the two first-year classes; 35 students in one class and 29 students in the other. The tests had been scored by computer, and an internal consistency reliability coefficient of .78 had been found for the entire group. The counselor, however, was interested in the classes separately, and, therefore, calculated the reliability coefficients for each class.
    The counselor would expect the reliability coefficients for the separate classes to be _____ 78.

    A. lower than
    B. about the same as

C. higher than
D. insufficient information is provided to make an estimate

13. A counselor was reviewing pre-workshop *parenting knowledge* test data from a group of 40 couples (i.e., 80 respondents) who would soon be participating in a five-session workshop on parenting. The counselor observed that the local group's mean was essentially the same as the national mean but that there was a negative skew in the local group's test data.
The counselor correctly reported to the workshop participants that

    A. they, as a group, tended to be below average in parenting knowledge
    B. they, as a group, tended to be above average in parenting knowledge
    C. there was an error in scoring the test
    D. some participants could not benefit from participation in the workshop

13.____

14. A respondent took a standardized aptitude test which yielded percentile ranks for three normative groups. The respondent's results were as follows: 55th percentile for local norms, 69th percentile for state norms, and 61st percentile for national norms. A counselor interpreting these data could correctly conclude that

    A. similar respondent aptitude in the state is generally higher than local respondent aptitude
    B. similar respondent aptitude nationally is lower than respondent aptitude locally
    C. similar respondent aptitude nationally is lower than respondent aptitude in the state
    D. no valid comparisons among the respective distributions can be made from these data

14.____

15. In analyzing response data from a test, one type of information considered to be important in evaluating the test is the percentages of respondents who answered each item correctly.
This percentage is known as the item _____ index.

    A. discrimination   B. parameter
    C. proportionality   D. difficulty

15.____

16. Person A and Person B both took the same test. Person A got a score of 100 while Person B got a score of 75.
In order for a counselor to determine whether the difference between their scores was because of *chance,* the counselor would need to know which of the following characteristics of the test?

    A. Mean
    B. Standard deviation
    C. Standard error of measurement
    D. Standard error of the mean

16.____

17. A person got a score of 83 on a norm-referenced test. This means that the person

    A. mastered 83% of the material covered in the test
    B. achieved a score better than 83% of those taking the test
    C. answered 83 questions correctly
    D. sufficient information has not been provided to answer the question

17.____

18. A measure that is highly reliable can be depended on to

    A. be equivalent
    B. measure accurately
    C. give consistent results
    D. be specific

19. A client's _____ is a number that indicates how many persons taking the same test performed worse than or equal to the client.

    A. norm
    B. percentile rank
    C. rank equivalent
    D. test rank

20. If several raters report a high degree of agreement in assessing a person, their ratings could be characterized as having a high degree of

    A. validity
    B. identity
    C. discrimination
    D. reliability

21. A counselor is conducting a study wherein observers are rating frequency of aggressive behavior among a group of children in a play counseling group. Most of the children are neatly dressed and well groomed, but a very few are untidy and disheveled.
    If the observers' ratings are biased because they psychologically equate untidiness and aggressive behavior, it would be an example of the _____ effect in research.

    A. Hawthorne
    B. placebo
    C. multiple treatment
    D. halo

22. A standard deviation is a measure of

    A. discrepancy
    B. variability
    C. covariability
    D. stability

23. A counseling researcher computed a Pearson product-moment correlation coefficient of +.71 between the Graduate Record Examination Total (GRET) scores and the Graduate Grade-Point Averages (GGPA) of a group of 28 students in a counselor education program.
    The researcher correctly concluded that

    A. approximately half of whatever was being measured by GGPA also was being measured by GRET for that group of students
    B. the correlation coefficient was not statistically significant
    C. it would have been better to correlate separately the GRE Verbal and Quantitative subsection scores with GGPA
    D. a larger sample was needed to validly determine the correlation between the variables

24. A counseling researcher completed a study, the essence of which was that clients' ratings of counseling effectiveness were positively and statistically significantly related to counselors' frequencies of use of active listening (i.e., facilitative responding) skills. The counselor then wrote a manuscript describing the study and its results and implications, and submitted copies of it to the JOURNAL OF COUNSELING AND DEVELOPMENT, COUNSELOR EDUCATION AND SUPERVISION, and THE JOURNAL OF COUNSELING PSYCHOLOGY.
    The counselor was MOST likely to

    A. have the manuscript accepted for publication very soon

B. have the manuscript rejected because the findings were *old news* in the counseling profession
C. be advised to restructure the manuscript into a *brief report* format
D. be charged with violation of AACD's ethical standards and NBCC's code of ethics

25. A counseling researcher conducted a study in which adult males and females who had exhibited symptoms of depression were randomly assigned to one of three treatment conditions: (a) individual counseling, (b) group counseling, or (c) family counseling. For each condition, the counseling intervention was conducted for at least six weeks, at which time the Beck Depression Inventory was administered to the subjects. The researcher was particularly interested in *treatment x gender* interaction effects. Therefore, the researcher would be BEST advised to conduct a(n) _____ analysis of variance.

    A. one-way
    B. factorial
    C. multivariate
    D. bi-level

26. A counselor conducted a study intended to evaluate the effectiveness of ongoing group career counseling on the vocational maturity of high school sophomores. The study was begun in September and continued until June. This study is particularly susceptible to which of the following threats to the validity of an experiment?

    A. Regression
    B. Maturation
    C. Reactive effects of experimentation
    D. Multiple treatment interference

27. A counselor designs a study where two experimental groups and one control group complete pre- and post-experiment measures of self-concept. The subjects were not randomly assigned to the groups because of scheduling problems.
    Which of the following techniques is MOST appropriate for analyzing the resultant data?

    A. Analysis of covariance
    B. Correlated t-tests
    C. Analysis of variance
    D. Wilcoxon matched-pairs signed-ranks test

28. If a theory covers a maximum of facts with a minimum of assumptions, it is referred to as being

    A. verifiable
    B. abstract
    C. concrete
    D. parsimonious

29. What would be the dependent variable in the statement *A rolling stone gathers no moss*?

    A. No
    B. Stone
    C. Moss
    D. Rolling

30. With which of the following types of experimental validity is the counseling researcher concerned when attempting to generalize research findings to other circumstances and subjects?

    A. Internal
    B. External
    C. Deductive
    D. Inductive

31. The Code of Ethics and the Ethical Standards of the American Association for Counseling and Development do NOT include a statement reflecting the principle that

   A. counselors have a right to protect clients from themselves if the clients give evidence of being self-injurious
   B. revelation of a counselor's notes on a client should not be made to other professionals unless the client has provided written permission to do so or the information has been subpoenaed by a court of law
   C. counselors should receive appropriate fees for services rendered regardless of the situations or settings in which the services were rendered
   D. improvement of the profession through a variety of professional involvements is a responsibility of all counselors

32. The state in which you reside does not yet have counselor licensure, so a local civic club has asked you to address their members to present an overview of counselor licensure and its benefits to the public.
In your presentation to the group, you note that

   A. licensure automatically entitles counselors to receive third-party payments from insurance companies
   B. some professional groups (e.g., psychologists) have opposed counselor licensure although the need for mental health services for the public has increased steadily
   C. state-level counselor licensure laws have existed for over twenty years although it is only recently that a majority of the states have counselor licensure laws
   D. one of the ways that counselor licensure laws protect the public's general welfare is through restriction of the use of the term *counselor* to those persons who have graduated from counselor education programs

33. A married couple comes to you, as a counselor in private practice, and tells you that they are having marital difficulties and have sought counseling for resolution of them. In the course of an initial session with them, one of the spouses reports being a new and active member of the local Alcoholics Anonymous (AA) group.
You should

   A. investigate the nature of the local AA's activities and continue counseling if those activities do not include accepted definitions of counseling
   B. terminate counseling with the one spouse but continue to work with the spouse who is not an AA participant
   C. offer to co-counsel with the staff of the local AA
   D. refer both spouses to the local AA

34. The Council for Accreditation of Counseling and Related Educational Programs (CACREP) STANDARDS FOR PREPARATION

   A. constitute the legal basis for certification and licensure requirements for professional counselors
   B. specify the minimum professional competencies (i.e., skills) which a counselor is expected to possess
   C. have been adopted by more than 60% of the approximately 480 counselor preparation programs in the United States
   D. are a set of guidelines for the desirable elements of and experiences in counselor preparation programs

35. A member of the local clergy telephones and asks for your evaluation of the moral values of a person whom the caller knows was one of your clients. The caller wants your opinion because the former client is an applicant to a theological institution for which the caller is the local applicant evaluator.
You should

   A. respond orally but require that no records be made of the conversation and that no comments be attributed to you
   B. inform the caller that under no circumstances are you ethically permitted to divulge the information requested
   C. inform the caller that you need to call the former client and obtain the client's permission before you can express your opinions
   D. seek the counsel of your supervisor to determine what types of information it would be permissible to divulge

36. You have been providing career counseling to a client who is seeking employment. Concurrent with the counseling, and with your knowledge, the client has made application for employment with several employers. A potential employer calls you and asks for your opinion as to your client's suitability for the employer's job opening.
Under which of the following conditions are you free (i.e., not in violation of professional ethics) to provide the information requested?

   A. When it is clear that the client will not get the job unless the information is given
   B. When you are certain that the information you would provide would assure that the client would get the job
   C. When in your best judgment you believe the information would enhance the client's chances for getting the job
   D. None of the above

37. As applied to professional licensure of counselors, the term *reciprocity* means that

   A. one licensing agency agrees to accept the licensing standards of another as sufficient for its own
   B. a licensed counselor may legally perform the functions of a licensed psychologist
   C. certification is synonymous with licensure
   D. graduation from a fully accredited counselor education program automatically constitutes eligibility for licensure

38. The publication that is likely to average the largest number of current research articles on the counseling process is the

   A. JOURNAL OF COUNSELING PSYCHOLOGY
   B. REVIEW OF EDUCATIONAL RESEARCH
   C. JOURNAL OF CONSULTING AND ABNORMAL PSYCHOLOGY
   D. JOURNAL OF NERVOUS AND MENTAL DISEASES

39. According to the Code of Ethics, when should a counselor try to persuade the client to report knowledge of a crime to the appropriate law enforcement authorities?

   A. When there is imminent danger to others
   B. When there is a crime in progress
   C. After the crime
   D. Never

40. Third-party reimbursement is a term pertinent to
    A. transactional analysis
    B. behavioral therapy
    C. insurance practices
    D. veterans' educational programs

40.____

KEY (CORRECT ANSWERS)

1. C	11. D	21. D	31. C
2. A	12. A	22. B	32. B
3. B	13. B	23. A	33. A
4. D	14. B	24. D	34. D
5. B	15. D	25. B	35. C
6. B	16. C	26. B	36. D
7. A	17. D	27. A	37. A
8. C	18. C	28. D	38. A
9. C	19. B	29. C	39. A
10. D	20. D	30. B	40. C

EXAMINATION SECTION
TEST 1

DIRECTIONS: Each question or incomplete statement is followed by several suggested answers or completions. Select the one that BEST answers the question or completes the statement. *PRINT THE LETTER OF IN THE CORRECT ANSWER THE SPACE AT THE RIGHT.*

1. Reports show that more men than women are physically handicapped MAINLY because

    A. women are instinctively more cautious than men
    B. men are more likely to have congenital deformities
    C. women tend to seek surgical remedies because of greater concern over personal appearance
    D. men have lower ability to recover from injury
    E. men are more likely to be exposed to hazardous conditions

2. Of the following, the explanation married women give MOST frequently for seeking employment outside the home is that they wish to

    A. escape the drudgeries of home life
    B. develop secondary employment skills
    C. maintain an emotionally satisfying career
    D. provide the main support for the family
    E. supplement the family income

3. Of the following home conditions, the one *most likely* to cause emotional disturbances in children is

    A. increased birthrate following the war
    B. disrupted family relationships
    C. lower family income than that of neighbors
    D. higher family income than that of neighbors
    E. overcrowded living conditions

4. Casual unemployment, as distinguished from other types of unemployment, is traceable MOST readily to

    A. a decrease in the demand for labor as a result of scientific progress
    B. more or less haphazard changes in the demand for labor in certain industries
    C. periodic changes in the demand for labor in certain industries
    D. disturbances and disruptions in industry resulting from international trade barriers
    E. increased mobility of the population

5. Labor legislation, although primarily intended for the benefit of the employee, MAY aid the employer by

    A. increasing his control over the immediate labor market
    B. prohibiting government interference with operating policies
    C. protecting him, through equalization of labor costs, from being undercut by other employers
    D. transferring to the general taxpayer the principal costs of industrial hazards of accident and unemployment
    E. increasing the pensions of civil service employees

6. When employment and unemployment figures both decline, the MOST probable conclusion is that

   A. the population has reached a condition of equilibrium
   B. seasonal employment has ended
   C. the labor force has decreased
   D. payments for unemployment insurance have been increased
   E. industrial progress has reduced working hours

7. An individual with an I.Q. of 100 may be said to have demonstrated _____ intelligence.

   A. superior
   B. absolute
   C. substandard
   D. approximately average
   E. high average

8. While state legislatures differ in many respects, all of them are *most nearly* alike in

   A. provisions for retirement of members
   B. rate of pay
   C. length of legislative sessions
   D. method of selection of their members
   E. length of term of office

9. If a state passed a law in a field under Congressional jurisdiction and if Congress subsequently passed contrary legislation, the state provision would be

   A. regarded as never having existed
   B. valid until the next session of the state legislature, which would be obliged to repeal it
   C. superseded by the federal statute
   D. ratified by Congress
   E. still operative in the state involved

10. Power to pardon offenses committed against the people of the United States is vested in the

    A. Supreme Court of the United States
    B. United States District Courts
    C. Federal Bureau of Investigation
    D. United States Parole Board
    E. President of the United States

11. As distinguished from formal social control of an individual's behavior, an example of informal social control is that exerted by

    A. public opinion
    B. religious doctrine
    C. educational institutions
    D. statutes
    E. public health measures

12. The PRINCIPAL function of the jury in a jury trial is to decide questions of

    A. equity
    B. fact
    C. injunction
    D. contract
    E. law

13. Of the following rights of an individual, the one which usually depends on citizenship as distinguished from those given anyone living under the laws of the United States is the right to

    A. receive public assistance
    B. hold an elective office
    C. petition the government for redress of grievances
    D. receive equal protection of the laws
    E. be accorded a trial by jury

14. If the characteristics of a person were being studied by competent observers, it would be expected that their observations would differ MOST markedly with respect to their evaluation of the person's

    A. intelligence
    B. nutritional condition
    C. temperamental characteristics
    D. weight
    E. height

15. If there are evidences of dietary deficiency in families where cereals make up a major portion of the diet, the *most likely* reason for this deficiency is that

    A. cereals cause absorption of excessive quantities of water
    B. persons who concentrate their diet on cereals do not chew their food properly
    C. carbohydrates are deleterious
    D. other essential food elements are omitted
    E. children eat cereals too rapidly

16. Although malnutrition is generally associated with poverty, dietary studies of population groups in the United States reveal that

    A. malnutrition is most often due to a deficiency of nutrients found chiefly in high-cost foods
    B. there has been overemphasis of the casual relationship between poverty and malnutrition
    C. malnutrition is found among people with sufficient money to be well fed
    D. a majority of the population in all income groups is undernourished
    E. malnutrition is not a factor in the incidence of rickets

17. The organization which has as one of its primary functions the mitigation of suffering caused by famine, fire, floods, and other national calamities is the

    A. National Safety Council
    B. Salvation Army
    C. Public Administration Service
    D. American National Red Cross
    E. American Legion

18. The MAIN difference between public welfare and private social agencies is that in public agencies,

   A. case records are open to the public
   B. the granting of assistance cannot be sufficiently flexible to meet the varying needs of individual recipients
   C. only financial assistance may be provided
   D. all policies and procedures must be based upon statutory authorizations
   E. economical and efficient administration are stressed because their funds are obtained through public taxation

18.___

19. A recipient of relief who is in need of the services of an attorney but is unable to pay the customary fees, should *generally* be referred to the

   A. Small Claims Court
   B. Domestic Relations Court
   C. County Lawyers Association
   D. City Law Department
   E. Legal Aid Society

19.___

20. An injured workman should file his claim for workmen's compensation with the

   A. State Labor Relations Board
   B. Division of Placement and Unemployment Insurance
   C. State Industrial Commission
   D. Workmen's Compensation Board
   E. State Insurance Board

20.___

21. The type of insurance found MOST frequently among families such as those assisted by the Department of Social Services is

   A. accident   B. straight life
   C. endowment   D. industrial
   E. personal liability

21.___

22. Of the following items in the standard budget of the Department of Social Services, the one for which actual expenditures would be MOST constant throughout the year is

   A. fuel   B. housing
   C. medical care   D. clothing
   E. household replacements

22.___

23. The MOST frequent cause of "broken homes" is attributed to the

   A. temperamental incompatibilities of parents and in-laws
   B. extension of the system of children's courts
   C. psychopathic irresponsibility of the parents
   D. institutionalization of one of the spouses
   E. death of one or both spouses

23.___

24. In rearing children, the problems of the widower are usually greater than those of the widow, largely because of the

    A. tendency of widowers to impose excessively rigid moral standards
    B. increased economic hardship
    C. added difficulty of maintaining a desirable home
    D. possibility that a stepmother will be added to the household
    E. prevalent masculine prejudice against pursuits which are inherently feminine

25. Foster-home placement of children is often advocated in preference to institutionalization *primarily* because

    A. the law does not provide for local supervision of children's institutions
    B. institutions furnish a more expensive type of care
    C. the number of institutions is insufficient compared to the number of children needing care
    D. children are not well treated in institutions
    E. foster homes provide a more normal environment for children

KEY (CORRECT ANSWERS)

1.	E	11.	A
2.	E	12.	B
3.	B	13.	B
4.	B	14.	C
5.	C	15.	D
6.	C	16.	C
7.	D	17.	D
8.	D	18.	D
9.	C	19.	E
10.	E	20.	D

21. D
22. B
23. E
24. C
25. E

TEST 2

DIRECTIONS: Each question or incomplete statement is followed by several suggested answers or completions. Select the one that BEST answers the question or completes the statement. *PRINT THE LETTER OF THE CORRECT ANSWER IN THE SPACE AT THE RIGHT.*

1. Of the following, the category MOST likely to yield the greatest reduction in cost to the taxpayer under improved employment conditions is

    A. home relief, including aid to the homeless
    B. aid to the blind
    C. aid to dependent children
    D. old-age assistance

    1.___

2. One of the MOST common characteristics of the chronic alcoholic is

    A. low intelligence level
    B. wanderlust
    C. psychosis
    D. egocentricity

    2.___

3. Of the following factors leading toward the cure of the alcoholic, the MOST important is thought to be

    A. removal of all alcohol from the immediate environment
    B. development of a sense of personal adequacy
    C. social disapproval of drinking
    D. segregation from former companions

    3.___

4. The Federal Housing Administration is the agency which

    A. insures mortgages made by lending institutions for new construction or remodeling of old construction
    B. provides federal aid for state and local government for slum clearance and housing for very low income families
    C. subsidizes the building industry through direct grants
    D. provides for the construction of low-cost housing projects owned and operated by the federal government

    4.___

5. In comparing the advantages of foster home over institutional placement, it is generally agreed that institutional care is LEAST advisable for children

    A. who cannot sustain the intimacy of foster family living because of their experiences with their own parents
    B. who are socially well-adjusted or have had considerable experience in living with a family
    C. who have need for special facilities for observation, diagnosis, and treatment
    D. whose natural parents find it difficult to accept the idea of foster home placement because of its close resemblance to adoption

    5.___

6. The school can play a vital part in detecting the child who displays overt symptomatic behavior indicative of social maladjustment CHIEFLY because the teacher has the opportunity to

   A. assume a pseudo-parental role in regard to discipline and punishment, thereby limiting the extent of the maladjusted child's anti-social behavior
   B. observe how the child relates to the group and what reactions are stimulated in him by his peer relationships
   C. determine whether the adjustment difficulties displayed by the child were brought on by the teacher herself or by the other students
   D. help the child's parents to resolve the difficulties in adjustment which are indicated by the child's reactions to the social pressures exerted by his peers

6.____

7. In treating juvenile delinquents, it has been found that there are some who make better social adjustment through group treatment than through an individual casework approach.
   In selecting delinquent boys for group treatment, the one of the following which is the MOST important consideration is that

   A. the boys to be treated in one group be friends or from the same community
   B. only boys who consent to group treatment be included in the group
   C. the ages of the boys included in the group vary as much as possible
   D. only boys who have not reacted to an individual casework approach be included in the group

7.____

8. Multi-problem families are generally characterized by various functional indicators.
   Of the following, the family which is *most likely* to be a multi-problem family is one which has

   A. unemployed adult family members
   B. parents with diagnosed character disorders
   C. children and parents with a series of difficulties in the community
   D. poor housekeeping standards

8.____

9. Multi-problem families generally have a complex history of intervention by a variety of social agencies.
   Of the following phases involved in planning for their treatment, the one which is MOST important to consider FIRST is the

   A. joint decision to limit any help to be given
   B. analysis of facts and definition of the problems involved
   C. determination of treatment priorities
   D. study of available community resources

9.____

10. The development of good public relations in the area for which the supervisor is responsible should be considered by the supervisor as

    A. not his responsibility as he is primarily responsible for his workers' services
    B. dependent upon him as he is in the best position to interpret the department to the community
    C. not important to the adequate functioning of the department
    D. a part of his method of carrying out his job responsibility as what his workers do affects the community

11. Of the following, the LEAST accurate statement concerning the relationship of public and private social agencies is that

    A. both have an important and necessary function to perform
    B. they are not to be considered as competing or rival agencies
    C. they are cooperating agencies
    D. their work is based on fundamentally different social work concepts

12. Of the following, the LEAST accurate statement concerning the worker-client relationship is that the worker should have the ability to

    A. express warmth of feeling in appropriate ways as a basis for a professional relationship which creates confidence
    B. feel appropriately in the relationship without losing the ability to see the situation in the perspective necessary to help the people immersed in it
    C. identify himself with the client so that the worker's personality does not influence the client
    D. use keen observation and perceive what is significant with a new range of appreciation of the meaning of the situation to the client

13. Of the following, the MOST fundamental psychological concept underlying case work in the public assistance field is that

    A. eligibility for public assistance should be reviewed from time to time
    B. workers should be aware of the prevalence of psychological disabilities among members of families on public assistance
    C. workers should realize the necessity of carrying out the policies laid down by the state office in order that state aid may be received
    D. in the process of receiving assistance, recipients should not be deprived of their normal status of self-direction

14. Of the following, the MOST comprehensive as well as the MOST accurate statement concerning the professional attitude of the social worker is that he should

    A. have a real concern for, and an intelligent interest in, the welfare of the client
    B. recognize that the client's feelings rather than the realities of his needs are of major importance to the client
    C. put at the client's service the worker's knowledge and sincere interest in him
    D. use his insight and understanding to make sound decisions about the client

15. The one of the following reasons for refusing a job which is LEAST acceptable, from the viewpoint of maintaining a client's continued rights to unemployment insurance benefits, is that

    A. acceptance of the job would interfere with the client's joining or retaining membership in a labor union
    B. there is a strike, lockout, or other industrial controversy in the establishment where employment is offered
    C. the distance from the place of employment to his home is greater than seems justified to the client
    D. the wages offered are lower than the prevailing wages in that locality

16. Experience pragmatically suggests that dislocation from cultural roots and customs makes for tension, insecurity, and anxiety. This holds for the child as well as the adolescent, for the new immigrant as well as the second-generation citizen.
    Of the following, the MOST important implication of the above statement for a social worker in any setting is that

    A. anxiety, distress, and incapacity are always personal and can be understood best only through an understanding of the child's present cultural environment
    B. in order to resolve the conflicts caused by the displacement of a child from a home with one cultural background to one with another, it is essential that the child fully replace his old culture with the new one
    C. no treatment goal can be envisaged for a dislocated child which does not involve a value judgment which is itself culturally determined
    D. anxiety and distress result from a child's reaction to culturally oriented treatment goals

17. Accepting the fact that mentally gifted children represent superior heredity, the United States faces an important eugenic problem CHIEFLY because

    A. unless these mentally gifted children mature and reproduce more rapidly than the less intelligent children, the nation is heading for a lowering of the average intelligence of its people
    B. although the mentally gifted child always excels scholastically, he generally has less physical stamina than the normal child and tends to lower the nation's population physically
    C. the mentally subnormal are increasing more rapidly than the mentally gifted in America, thus affecting the overall level of achievement of the gifted child
    D. unless the mental level of the general population is raised to that of the gifted child, the mentally gifted will eventually usurp the reigns of government and dominate the mentally weaker

18. The form of psychiatric treatment which requires the LEAST amount of participation on the part of the patient is

    A. psychoanalysis   B. psychotherapy
    C. shock therapy   D. non-directive therapy

19. Tests administered by psychologists for the PRIMARY purpose of measuring intelligence are known as _____ tests.

    A. projective
    B. validating
    C. psychometric
    D. apperception

20. In recent years, there have been some significant changes in the treatment of patients in state psychiatric hospitals. These changes are PRIMARILY caused by the use of

    A. electric shock therapy
    B. tranquilizing drugs
    C. steroids
    D. the open-ward policy

21. The psychological test which makes use of a set of twenty pictures, each depicting a dramatic scene, is known as the

    A. Goodenough Test
    B. Thematic Apperception Test
    C. Minnesota Multiphasic Personality Inventory
    D. Healy Picture Completion Test

22. One of the MOST effective ways in which experimental psychologists have been able to study the effects on personality of heredity and environment has been through the study of

    A. primitive cultures
    B. identical twins
    C. mental defectives
    D. newborn infants

23. In hospitals with psychiatric divisions, the psychiatric function is PREDOMINANTLY that of

    A. the training of personnel in all psychiatric disciplines
    B. protection of the community against potentially dangerous psychiatric patients
    C. research and study of psychiatric patients so that new knowledge and information can be made generally available
    D. short-term hospitalization designed to determine diagnosis and recommendations for treatment

24. Predictions of human behavior on the basis of past behavior frequently are INACCURATE because

    A. basic patterns of human behavior are in a continual state of flux
    B. human behavior is not susceptible to explanation of a scientific nature
    C. the underlying psychological mechanisms of behavior are not completely understood
    D. quantitative techniques for the measurement of stimuli and responses are unavailable

25. Socio-cultural factors are being re-evaluated in casework practice as they influence both the worker and the client in their participation in the casework process.
Of the following factors, the one which is currently being studied MOST widely is the

   A. social class of worker and client and its significance in casework
   B. difference in native intelligence which can be ascribed to racial origin of an individual
   C. cultural values affecting the areas in which an individual functions
   D. necessity in casework treatment of the client's membership in an organized religious group

25._____

KEY (CORRECT ANSWERS)

1. A	11. D
2. D	12. C
3. B	13. D
4. A	14. C
5. B	15. C
6. B	16. C
7. B	17. A
8. C	18. C
9. B	19. C
10. D	20. B

21. B
22. B
23. D
24. C
25. C

EXAMINATION SECTION
TEST 1

DIRECTIONS: Each question or incomplete statement is followed by several suggested answers or completions. Select the one that BEST answers the question or completes the statement. *PRINT THE LETTER OF THE CORRECT ANSWER IN THE SPACE AT THE RIGHT.*

1. Deviant behavior is a sociological term used to describe behavior which is not in accord with generally accepted standards. This may include juvenile delinquency, adult criminality, mental or physical illness.
   Comparison of normal with deviant behavior is useful to social workers because it

   A. makes it possible to establish watertight behavioral descriptions
   B. provides evidence of differential social behavior which distinguishes deviant from normal behavior
   C. indicates that deviant behavior is of no concern to social workers
   D. provides no evidence that social role is a determinant of behavior

2. Alcoholism may affect an individual client's ability to function as a spouse, parent, worker, and citizen.
   A social worker's MAIN responsibility to a client with a history of alcoholism is to

   A. interpret to the client the causes of alcoholism as a disease syndrome
   B. work with the alcoholic's family to accept him as he is and stop trying to reform him
   C. encourage the family of the alcoholic to accept casework treatment
   D. determine the origins of his particular drinking problem, establish a diagnosis, and work out a treatment plan for him

3. There is a trend to regard narcotic addiction as a form of illness for which the current methods of intervention have not been effective.
   Research on the combination of social, psychological, and physical causes of addiction would indicate that social workers should

   A. oppose hospitalization of addicts in institutions
   B. encourage the addict to live normally at home
   C. recognize that there is no successful treatment for addiction and act accordingly
   D. use the existing community facilities differentially for each addict

4. A study of social relationships among delinquent and non-delinquent youth has shown that

   A. delinquent youth generally conceal their true feelings and maintain furtive social contacts
   B. delinquents are more impulsive and vivacious than law-abiding boys
   C. non-delinquent youths diminish their active social relationships in order to sublimate any anti-social impulses
   D. delinquent and non-delinquent youths exhibit similar characteristics of impulsiveness and vivaciousness

5. The one of the following which is the CHIEF danger of interpreting the delinquent behavior of a child in terms of morality *alone* when attempting to get at its causes is that

   A. this tends to overlook the likelihood that the causes of the child's actions are more than a negation of morality and involve varied symptoms of disturbance
   B. a child's moral outlook toward life and society is largely colored by that of his parents, thus encouraging parent-child conflict
   C. too careful a consideration of the moral aspects of the offense and of the child's needs may often negate the demands of justice in a case
   D. standards of morality may be of no concern to the delinquent and he may not realize the seriousness of his offenses

6. Experts in the field of personnel administration are generally agreed that an employee should not be under the immediate supervision of more than one supervisor. A certain worker, because of an emergency situation, divides his time equally between two limited caseloads on a prearranged time schedule. Each unit has a different supervisor, and the worker performs substantially the same duties in each caseload.
   The above statement is pertinent in this situation CHIEFLY because

   A. each supervisor, feeling that the cases in her unit should have priority, may demand too much of the worker's time
   B. the two supervisors may have different standards of work performance and may prefer different methods of doing the work
   C. the worker works part-time on each caseload and may not have full knowledge or control of the situation in either caseload
   D. the task of evaluating the worker's services will be doubled, with two supervisors instead of one having to rate his work

7. Experts in modern personnel management generally agree that employees on all job levels should be permitted to offer suggestions for improving work methods.
   Of the following, the CHIEF limitation of such suggestions is that they may, at times,

   A. be offered primarily for financial reward and not show genuine interest in improvement of work methods
   B. be directed towards making individual jobs easier
   C. be restricted by the employees' fear of radically changing the work methods favored by their supervisors
   D. show little awareness of the effects on the overall objectives and functions of the entire agency

8. Through the supervisory process and relationship, the supervisor is trying to help workers gain increased self-awareness.
   Of the following statements concerning this process, the one which is MOST accurate is:

   A. Self-awareness is developed gradually so that worker can learn to control his own reactions.
   B. Worker is expected to be introspective primarily for his own enlightenment.
   C. Supervisor is trying to help worker handle any emotional difficulties he may reveal.
   D. Worker is expected at the onset to share and determine with the supervisor what in his previous background makes it difficult for him to use certain ideas.

9. The one of the following statements concerning principles in the learning process which is LEAST accurate is:

   A. Some degree of regression on the part of the worker is usually natural in the process of development and this should be accepted by the supervisor.
   B. When a beginning worker shows problems, the supervisor should first handle this behavior as a personality difficulty.
   C. It has been found in the work training process that some degree of resistance is usually inevitable.
   D. The emotional content of work practice may tend to set up *blind spots* in workers.

10. Of the following, the one that represents the BEST basis for planning the content of a successful staff development program is the

    A. time available for meetings
    B. chief social problems of the community
    C. common needs of the staff workers as related to the situations with which they are dealing
    D. experimental programs conducted by other agencies

11. In planning staff development seminars, the MOST valuable topics for discussion are likely to be those selected from

    A. staff suggestions based on the staff's interest and needs
    B. topics recommended for consideration by professional organizations
    C. topics selected by the administration based on demonstrated limitations of staff skill and knowledge
    D. topics selected by the administration based on a combination of staff interest and objectivity evaluated staff needs

12. Staff meetings designed to promote professional staff development are MOST likely to achieve this goal when

    A. there is the widest participation among all staff members who attend the meetings
    B. participation by the most skilled and experienced staff members is predominant
    C. participation by selected staff members is planned before the meeting sessions
    D. supervisory personnel take major responsibility for participation

13. Assume that you are the leader of a conference attended by representatives of various city and private agencies. After the conference has been underway for a considerable time, you realize that the representative of one of these agencies has said nothing.
    It would generally be BEST for you to

    A. ask him if he would like to say anything
    B. ask the group a pertinent question that he would probably be best able to answer
    C. make no special effort to include him in the conversation
    D. address the next question you planned to ask to him directly

14. A member of a decision-making conference generally makes his BEST contribution to the conference when he

    A. compromises on his own point of view and accepts most of the points of other conference members
    B. persuades the conference to accept all or most of his points

C. persuades the conference to accept his major proposals but will yield on the minor ones
D. succeeds in integrating his ideas with the ideas of the other conference members

15. Of the following, the LEAST accurate statement concerning the compilation and use of statistics in administration is:

    A. Interpretation of statistics is as necessary as their compilation.
    B. Statistical records of expenditures and services are one of the bases for budget preparation.
    C. Statistics on the quality of services rendered to the community will clearly delineate the human values achieved.
    D. The results achieved from collecting and compiling statistics must be in keeping with the cost and effort required.

16. An important administrative problem is how precisely to define the limits on authority that is delegated to subordinate supervisors.
    Such definition of limits of authority SHOULD be

    A. as precise as possible and practicable in all areas
    B. as precise as possible and practicable in all areas of function, but should allow considerable flexibility in the area of personnel management
    C. as precise as possible and practicable in the area of personnel management, but should allow considerable flexibility in the areas of function
    D. in general terms so as to allow considerable flexibility both in the areas of function and in the areas of personnel management

17. The LEAST important of the following reasons why a particular activity should be assigned to a unit which performs activities dissimilar to it is that

    A. close coordination is needed between the particular activity and other activities performed by the unit
    B. it will enhance the reputation and prestige of the unit supervisor
    C. the unit makes frequent use of the results of this particular activity
    D. the unit supervisor has a sound knowledge and understanding of the particular activity

18. The MOST important of the following reasons why the average resident of a deteriorated slum neighborhood resists relocation to an area in the suburbs with better physical accommodations is that he

    A. does not recognize as undesirable the characteristics which are responsible for deterioration of the neighborhood
    B. has some expectation of neighborly assistance in his old home in times of stress and adversity
    C. hopes for better days when he may be able to become a figure of some importance and envy in the old neighborhood
    D. is attuned to the noise of the city and fears the quiet of the suburb

19. From a psychological and sociological point of view, the MOST important of the following dangers to the persons living in an economically depressed area in which the only step taken by governmental and private social agencies to assist these persons is the granting of a dole is that

    A. industry will be reluctant to expand its operations in that area
    B. the dole will encourage additional non-producers to enter the area
    C. the residents of the area will probably have to find their own solution to their problems
    D. their permanent dependency will be fostered

20. The term *real wages* is GENERALLY used by economists to mean the

    A. amount of take-home pay left after taxes, social security, and other such deductions have been made by the employer
    B. average wage actually earned during a calendar or fiscal year
    C. family income expressed on a per capita basis
    D. wages expressed in terms of its buyer power

21. It has, at times, been suggested that an effective way to eradicate juvenile delinquency would be to arrest and punish the parents for the criminal actions of their delinquent children.
    The one of the following which is the CHIEF defect of this proposal is that

    A. it fails to get at the cause of the delinquent act and tends to further weaken disturbed parent-child relationships
    B. since the criminally inclined child has apparently demonstrated little love or affection for his parent, the child will be unlikely to amend his behavior in order to avoid hurting his parent
    C. the child who commits anti-social acts does so in many cases in order to hurt his parents so that this proposal would not only increase the parents' sorrow, but would also serve as an incentive to more delinquency by the child
    D. the punishment should be limited to the person who commits the illegal action rather than to those who are most interested in his welfare

22. Surveys which have compared the relative stability of marriages between white persons with marriages between non-white persons in this country have shown that, among Blacks, there is

    A. a significantly higher percentage of spouses absent from the household than among whites
    B. a significantly higher percentage of spouses absent from the household than among whites living in the South, but the opposite is true in the Northeast
    C. a significantly lower percentage of spouses absent from the household than among whites
    D. no significant difference in the percentage of spouses absent from the household when compared with the white population

23. A phenomenon found in the cultural and recreational patterns of European immigrant families in America is that, generally, the foreign-born adults

    A. as well as their children, tend soon to forget their old-world activities and adopt the cultural and recreational customs of America
    B. as well as their children, tend to retain and continue their old-world cultural and recreational pursuits, and find it equally difficult to adopt those of America
    C. tend soon to drop their old pursuits and adopt the cultural and recreational patterns of America while their children find it somewhat more difficult to make this change
    D. tend to retain and continue their old-world cultural and recreational pursuits while their children tend to rapidly replace these by the games and cultural patterns of America

24. Certain mores of migrant groups are strengthened under the impact of their contact with the native society while other mores are weakened.
    In the case of Puerto Ricans who have come to the city, the effect of such contact upon their traditional family structure has been a

    A. strengthening of the former maternalistic family structure
    B. strengthening of the former paternalistic family structure
    C. weakening of the former maternalistic family structure
    D. weakening of the former paternalistic family structure

25. Administrative reviews and special studies of independent experts, as reported by the Department of Health, Education and Welfare, indicate that the proportion of recipients of public assistance who receive such assistance through *wilful misrepresentation* of the facts is

    A. less than 1%
    B. about 4%
    C. between 4% and 7%
    D. between 7% and 10%

KEY (CORRECT ANSWERS)

1.	B	11.	D
2.	D	12.	A
3.	D	13.	B
4.	B	14.	D
5.	A	15.	C
6.	B	16.	A
7.	D	17.	B
8.	A	18.	B
9.	B	19.	D
10.	C	20.	D

21. A
22. A
23. D
24. D
25. A

TEST 2

DIRECTIONS: Each question or incomplete statement is followed by several suggested answers or completions. Select the one that BEST answers the question or completes the statement. *PRINT THE LETTER OF THE CORRECT ANSWER IN THE SPACE AT THE RIGHT.*

1. In order to meet more adequately the public assistance needs occasioned by sudden changes in the national economy, social service agencies, in general, recommend, as a matter of preference, that

    A. each locality build up reserve funds to care for needy unemployed persons in order to avoid a breakdown of local resources such as occurred during the depression
    B. the federal government assume total responsibility for the administration of public assistance
    C. state settlement laws be strictly enforced so that unemployed workers will be encouraged to move from the emergency industry centers to their former homes
    D. a federal-state-local program of general assistance be established with need as the only eligibility requirement
    E. eligibility requirements be tightened to assure that only legitimately worthy local residents receive the available assistance

1.____

2. The MOST practical method of maintaining income for the majority of aged persons who are no longer able to work, or for the families of those workers who are deceased, is a(n)

    A. comprehensive system of non-categorical assistance on a basis of cash payments
    B. integrated system of public assistance and extensive work relief programs
    C. co-ordinated system of providing care in institutions and foster homes
    D. system of contributory insurance in which a cash benefit is paid as a matter of right
    E. expanded system of diagnostic and treatment centers

2.____

3. With the establishment of insurance and assistance programs under the Social Security Act, many institutional programs for the aged have tended to the greatest extent toward an increased emphasis on providing, of the following types of assistance,

    A. care for the aged by denominational groups
    B. care for children requiring institutional treatment
    C. recreational facilities for the able-bodied aged
    D. training facilities in industrial homework for the aged
    E. care for the chronically ill and infirm aged

3.____

4. Of the following terms, the one which BEST describes the Social Security Act is

    A. enabling legislation
    B. regulatory statute
    C. appropriations act
    D. act of mandamus
    E. provisional enactment

4.____

117

5. Of the following, the term which MOST accurately describes an appropriation is

   A. authority to spend
   B. itemized estimate
   C. *fund* accounting
   D. anticipated expenditure
   E. executive budget

6. When business expansion causes a demand for labor, the worker group which benefits MOST immediately is the group comprising

   A. employed workers
   B. inexperienced workers under 21 years of age
   C. experienced workers 21 to 25 years of age
   D. inexperienced older workers
   E. experienced workers over 40 years of age

7. The MOST important failure in our present system of providing social work services in local communities is the

   A. absence of adequate facilities for treating mental illness
   B. lack of coordination of available data and service in the community
   C. poor quality of the casework services provided by the public agencies
   D. limitations of the probation and parole services
   E. inadequacy of private family welfare services

8. Recent studies of the relationship between incidence of illness and the use of available treatment services among various population groups in the United States show that

   A. while lower-income families use medical services with greater frequency, total expenditures are greater among the upper-income groups
   B. although the average duration of a period of medical care increases with increasing income, the average frequency of obtaining care decreases with increasing income
   C. adequacy of medical service is inversely related to frequency of illness and size of family income
   D. families in the higher-income brackets have a heavier incidence of illness and make greater use of medical services than do those in the lower-income brackets
   E. both as to frequency and duration, the distribution of illness falls equally on all groups, but the use of medical services increases with income

9. The category of disease which most public health departments and authorities usually are NOT equipped to handle *directly* is that of

   A. chronic disease
   B. bronchial disturbances
   C. venereal disease
   D. mosquito-borne diseases
   E. incipient forms of tuberculosis

10. Recent statistical analyses of the causes of death in the United States indicate that medical science has now reached the stage where it would be preferable to increase its research toward control, among the following, PRINCIPALLY of

   A. accidents
   B. suicides
   C. communicable disease
   D. chronic disease
   E. infant mortality

11. Although the distinction between mental disease and mental deficiency is fairly definite, both these conditions USUALLY represent

   A. diseases of one part or organ of the body rather than of the whole person
   B. an inadequacy existing from birth or shortly afterwards and appearing as a simplicity of intelligence
   C. a deficiency developing later in life and characterized by distortions of attitude and belief
   D. inadequacies in meeting life situations and in conducting one's affairs
   E. somewhat transitory conditions characterized by disturbances of consciousness

12. According to studies made by reliable medical research organizations in the United States, differences among the states in proportion of physicians to population are MOST directly related to the

   A. geographic resources among the states
   B. skill of the physicians
   C. relative proportions of urban and rural people in the population of the states
   D. number of specialists in the ranks of the physicians
   E. health status of the people in the various states

13. One of the MAIN advantages of incorporating a charitable organization is that

   A. gifts or property of a corporation cannot be held in perpetuity
   B. gifts to unincorporated charitable organizations are not deductible from the taxable income
   C. incorporation gives less legal standing or *personality* than an informal partnership
   D. members of a corporation cannot be held liable for debts contracted by the organization
   E. a corporate organization cannot be sued

14. The BASIC principle underlying a social security program is that the government should provide

   A. aid to families that is not dependent on state or local participation
   B. assistance to any worthy family unable to maintain itself independently
   C. protection to individuals against some of the social risks that are inherent in an industrialized society
   D. safeguards against those factors leading to economic depression

15. The activities of state and local public welfare agencies are dependent to a large degree on the public assistance program of the federal government.
    The one of the following which the federal government has NOT been successful in achieving within the local agencies is the

    A. broadening of the scope of public assistance administration
    B. expansion of the categorical programs
    C. improvement of the quality of service given to clients
    D. standardization of the administration of general assistance programs

16. Of the following statements, the one which BEST describes the federal government's position, as stated in the Social Security Act, with regard to tests of character or fitness to be administered by local or state welfare departments to prospective clients is that

    A. no tests of character are required but they are not specifically prohibited
    B. if tests of character are used, they must be uniform throughout the state
    C. tests of character are contrary to the philosophy of the federal government and are to be considered illegal
    D. no tests of character are required, and assistance to those states that use them will be withheld

17. An increase in the size of the welfare grant may increase the cost of the welfare program not only in terms of those already on the welfare rolls, but because it may result in an increase in the number of people on the rolls.
    The CHIEF reason that an increase in the size of the grant may cause an increase in the number of people on the rolls is that the increased grant may

    A. induce low-salaried wage earners to apply for assistance rather than continue at their menial jobs
    B. make eligible for assistance many people whose resources are just above the previous standard
    C. induce many people to apply for assistance who hesitated to do so because of meagerness of the previous grant
    D. make relatives less willing to contribute because the welfare grant can more adequately cover their dependents' needs

18. One of the MAIN differences between the use of casework methods by a public welfare agency and by a private welfare agency is that the public welfare agency

    A. requires that the applicant be eligible for the services it offers
    B. cannot maintain a non-judgmental attitude toward its clients because of legal requirements
    C. places less emphasis on efforts to change the behavior of its clients
    D. must be more objective in its approach to the client because public funds are involved

19. All definitions of social casework include certain major assumptions.
    Of the following, the one which is NOT considered a major assumption is that

    A. the individual and society are interdependent
    B. social forces influence behavior and attitudes, affording opportunity for self-development and contribution to the world in which we live
    C. reconstruction of the total personality and reorganization of the total environment are specific goals
    D. the client is a responsible participant at every step in the solution of his problems

20. In order to provide those services to problem families which will help restore them to a self-maintaining status, it is necessary to FIRST

    A. develop specific plans to meet the individual needs of the problem family
    B. reduce the size of those caseloads composed of multi-problem families
    C. remove them from their environment and provide them with the means of overcoming their dependency
    D. identify the factors causing their dependency and creating problems for them

21. Of the following, the type of service which can provide the client with the MOST enduring help is that service which

    A. provides him with material aid and relieves the stress of his personal problems
    B. assists him to do as much as he can for himself and leaves him free to make his own decisions
    C. directs his efforts towards returning to a self-maintaining status and provides him with desirable goals
    D. gives him the feeling that the agency is interested in him as an individual and stands ready to assist him with his problems

22. Psychiatric interpretation of unconscious motivations can bring childhood conflicts into the framework of adult understanding and open the way for them to be resolved, but the interpretation must come from within the client.
    This statement means MOST NEARLY that

    A. treatment is merely diagnosis in reverse
    B. explaining a client to himself will lead to the resolution of his problems
    C. the client must arrive at an understanding of his problems
    D. unresolved childhood conflicts create problems for the adult

23. A significant factor in the United States economic picture is the state of the labor market. Of the following, the MOST important development affecting the labor market has been

    A. an expansion of the national defense effort creating new plant capacity
    B. the general increase in personal income as a result of an increase in overtime pay in manufacturing industries
    C. the growth of manufacturing as a result of automation
    D. a demand for a large number of jobs resulting from new job applicants as well as from displacement of workers by automation

24. A typical characteristic of the United States population over 65 is that MOST of them

    A. are independent and capable of self-support
    B. live in their own homes but require various supportive services
    C. live in institutions for the aged
    D. require constant medical attention at home or in an institution

25. The one of the following factors which is MOST important in preventing persons 65 years of age and older from getting employment is the

    A. misconceptions by employers of skills and abilities of senior citizens
    B. lack of skill in modern industrial techniques of persons in this age group
    C. social security laws restricting employment of persons in this age group
    D. unwillingness of persons in this age group to continue supporting themselves

KEY (CORRECT ANSWERS)

1. D
2. D
3. E
4. A
5. A

6. B
7. B
8. C
9. A
10. D

11. D
12. C
13. D
14. C
15. D

16. A
17. B
18. C
19. C
20. D

21. B
22. C
23. D
24. B
25. A

EXAMINATION SECTION
TEST 1

DIRECTIONS: Each question or incomplete statement is followed by several suggested answers or completions. Select the one that *BEST* answers the question or completes the statement. *PRINT THE LETTER OF THE CORRECT ANSWER IN THE SPACE AT THE RIGHT.*

1. When a counselor is planning a future interview with a client, of the following, the *MOST* important consideration is the

    A. recommendations he will make to the client
    B. place where the client will be interviewed
    C. purpose for which the client will be interviewed
    D. personality of the client

2. For a counselor to make a practice of reviewing the client's case record, if available, prior to the interview, is, usually,

    A. *inadvisable,* because knowledge of the client's past record will tend to influence the counselor's judgment
    B. *advisable,* because knowledge of the client's background will help the counselor to identify discrepancies in the client's responses
    C. *inadvisable,* because such review is time-consuming and of questionable value
    D. *advisable,* because knowledge of the client's background will help the counselor to understand the client's situation

3. Assume that a counselor makes a practice of constantly reassuring clients with serious and complex problems by making such statements as: "I'm sure you'll soon be well;" "I know you'll get a job soon;" or "Everything will be all right."
   Of the following, the *MOST* likely result of such a practice is to

    A. encourage the client and make him feel that the counselor understands what the client is going through
    B. make the client doubtful about the counselor's understanding of his difficulties and the counselor's ability to help
    C. confuse the client and cause him to hesitate to take any action on his own initiative
    D. help the client to be more realistic about his situation and the probability that it will improve

4. In order to get the maximum amount of information from a client during an interview, of the following, it is *MOST* important for the counselor to communicate to the client the feeling that the counselor is

    A. interested in the client
    B. a figure of authority
    C. efficient in his work habits
    D. sympathetic to the client's lifestyle

5. Of the following, the counselor who takes extremely detailed notes during an interview with a client is *most likely* to

    A. encourage the client to talk freely

B. distract and antagonize the client
C. help the client feel at ease
D. understand the client's feelings

6. As a counselor, you find that many of the clients you interview are verbally abusive and unusually hostile to you.
   Of the following, the MOST appropriate action for you to take *first* is to

   A. review your interviewing techniques and consider whether you may be provoking these clients
   B. act in a more authoritative manner when interviewing troublesome clients
   C. tell these clients that you will not process their applications unless their troublesome behavior ceases
   D. disregard the clients' troublesome behavior during the interview

7. During an interview, you did not completely understand several of your client's responses. In each instance, you rephrased the client's statement and asked the client if that was what he meant.
   For you to use such a technique during interviews would be considered

   A. *inappropriate;* you may have distorted the client's meaning by rephrasing his statements
   B. *inappropriate;* you should have asked the same questioE until you received a comprehensible response
   C. *appropriate;* the client will have a chance to correct you if you have misinterpreted his responses
   D. *appropriate;* a counselor should rephrase clients' responses for the records

8. A counselor is interviewing a client who has just had a severe emotional shock because of an assault on her by a mugger.
   Of the following, the approach which would generally be MOST helpful to the client is for the counselor to

   A. comfort the client and encourage her to talk about the assault
   B. sympathize with the client but refuse to discuss the assault with her
   C. tell the client to control her emotions and think positively about the future
   D. proceed with the interview in an impersonal and unemotional manner

9. A counselor finds that her questions are misinterpreted by many of the clients she interviews.
   Of the following, the MOST likely reason for this problem is that the

   A. client is not listening attentively
   B. client wants to avoid the subject being discussed
   C. counselor has failed to express her meaning clearly
   D. counselor has failed to put the client at ease

10. For a counselor to look directly at the client and observe him during the interview is generally

    A. *inadvisable;* this will make the client nervous and uncomfortable
    B. *advisable;* the client will be more likely to refrain from lying
    C. *inadvisable;* the counselor will not be able to take notes for the case record
    D. *advisable;* this will encourage conversation and accelerate the progress of the interview

11. You are interviewing a client who is applying for social services for the first time. In order to encourage this client to freely give you the information needed for you to establish his eligibility, of the following, the BEST way to start the interview is by

    A. asking questions the client can easily answer
    B. conveying the impression that his responses to your questions will be checked
    C. asking two or three similar but important questions
    D. assuring the client that your sole responsibility is "getting the facts"

12. Counselors are encouraged to record significant information obtained from clients and services provided for clients. Of the following, the MOST important reason for this practice is that these case records will

    A. help to reduce the need for regular supervisory conferences
    B. indicate to counselors which clients are taking up the most time
    C. provide information which will help the agency to improve its services to clients
    D. make it easier to verify the complaints of clients

13. As a counselor you find that interviews can be completed in a shorter period of time if you ask questions which limit the client to a certain answer.
    For you to use such a technique would be considered

    A. *inappropriate,* because this type of question usually requires advance preparation
    B. *inappropriate,* because this type of question may inhibit the client from saying what he really means
    C. *appropriate,* because you know the areas into which the questions should be directed
    D. *appropriate,* because this type of question usually helps clients to express themselves clearly

14. Assume that, while you are interviewing an individual to obtain information, the individual pauses in the middle of an answer.
    The BEST of the following actions for you to take at this time is to

    A. correct any inaccuracies in what he has said
    B. remain silent until he continues
    C. explain your position on the matter being discussed
    D. explain that time is short and that he must complete his story quickly

15. You have been assigned to interview the mother of a five-year-old son in her home to get information useful in locating the child's absent father. During the interview, you notice many serious bruises on the child's arms and legs, which the mother explains are due to the child's clumsiness. Of the following, your BEST course of action is to

    A. accept the mother's explanation and concentrate on getting information which will help you to locate the father
    B. advise the mother to have the child examined for a medical condition that may be causing his clumsiness
    C. make a surprise visit to the mother later, to see if someone is beating the child
    D. complete your interview with the mother and report the case to your supervisor for investigation of possible child abuse

16. During an interview, the former landlord of an absent father offers to help you to locate the father if you will give the landlord confidential information you have on the financial situation of the father.
    Of the following, you should

    A. immediately end the interview with the landlord
    B. urge the landlord to help you but explain that you are not permitted to give him confidential information
    C. freely give the landlord the confidential information he requests about the father
    D. give the landlord the information only if he promises to keep it confidential

17. You feel that your client, a released mental patient, is not adjusting well to living on his own in an apartment. To gather more information, you interview privately his next-door neighbor, who claims that the client is creating a "disturbance" and speaks of the client in an angry and insulting manner.
    Of the following, the BEST action for you to take in this situation is to

    A. listen patiently to the neighbor to try to get the facts about your client's behavior
    B. inform the neighbor that he has no right to speak insultingly about a mentally ill person
    C. make an appointment to interview the neighbor some other time when he isn't so upset
    D. tell the neighbor that you were not aware of the client's behavior and that you will have the client moved

18. As a counselor, you are interviewing a client to determine his eligibility for a work program. Suddenly the client begins to shout that he is in no condition to work and that you are persecuting him for no reason.
    Of the following, your BEST response to this client is to

    A. advise the client to stop shouting or you will call for the security guard
    B. wait until the client calms down, then order him to come back for another interview
    C. insist that you are not persecuting the client and that he must complete the interview
    D. wait until the client calms down, say that you understand how he feels, and try to continue the interview

19. You are interviewing a mother whose 17-year-old son has recently been returned home from a mental institution. Although she is willing to care for her son at home, she is frightened by his strange and sometimes violent behavior and does not know the best arrangement to make for his care.
    Of the following, your MOST appropriate response to this mother's problem is to

    A. describe the supportive services and alternatives to home care which are available
    B. help her to accept her son's strange and violent behavior
    C. tell her that she will not be permitted to care for her son at home if she is frightened by his behavior
    D. convince her that she is not responsible for her son's mental condition

20. Assume that you are interviewing an elderly man who comes to the center several times a month to discuss topics with you which are not related to social services. You realize that the man is lonely and enjoys these conversations.
    Of the following, it would be MOST appropriate to

    A. politely discourage the man from coming in to pass the time with you
    B. avoid speaking to this man the next time he comes into the center
    C. explore with the client his feelings about joining a senior citizens' center
    D. continue to hold these conversations with the man

21. A client you are interviewing tends to ramble on after each response that he gives, so that many clients are kept waiting.
    In this situation, of the following, it would be MOST advisable to

    A. try to direct the interview, in order to obtain the necessary information
    B. reduce the number of questions asked so that you can shorten the interview
    C. arrange a second interview for the client so that you can give him more time
    D. tell the client that he is wasting everybody's time

22. A non-minority counselor is about to interview a minority client on public assistance for job placement when the client says: "What does your kind know about my problems? You've never had to survive out on these streets."
    Of the following, the counselor's MOST appropriate response in this situation is to

    A. postpone the interview until a minority counselor is available to interview the client
    B. tell the client that he must cooperate with the counselor if he wants to continue receiving public assistance
    C. explain to the client the function of the counselor in this unit and the services he provides
    D. assure the client that you do not have to be a member of a minority group to understand the effects of poverty

23. When you are interviewing someone to obtain information, the BEST of the following reasons for you to repeat certain of his exact words is to

    A. *assure* him that appropriate action will be taken
    B. *encourage* him to elaborate on a point he has made
    C. *assure* him that you agree with his point of view
    D. *encourage* him to switch to another topic of discussion

24. You are interviewing a young client who seriously under-estimates the amount of education and training he will require for a certain occupation.
    For you to tell the client that you think he is mistaken would generally be considered

    A. *inadvisable,* because counselors should not express their opinions to clients
    B. *inadvisable,* because clients have the right to self-determination
    C. *advisable,* because clients should generally be alerted to their misconceptions
    D. *advisable,* because counselors should convince clients to adopt a proper life style

25. Of the following, the MOST appropriate manner for a counselor to assume during an interview with a patient is

    A. authoritarian
    B. paternal
    C. casual
    D. businesslike

25.____

KEY (CORRECT ANSWERS)

1.	C	11.	A
2.	D	12.	C
3.	B	13.	B
4.	A	14.	B
5.	B	15.	D
6.	A	16.	B
7.	C	17.	A
8.	A	18.	D
9.	C	19.	A
10.	D	20.	C

21. A
22. C
23. B
24. C
25. D

TEST 2

DIRECTIONS: Each question or incomplete statement is followed by several suggested answers or completions. Select the one that *BEST* answers the question or completes the statement. *PRINT THE LETTER OF THE CORRECT ANSWER IN THE SPACE AT THE RIGHT.*

1. You are interviewing a legally responsible absent father who refuses to make child support payments because he claims the mother physically abuses the child.
   Of the following, the *BEST* way for you to handle this situation is to tell the father that you

   A. will report his complaint about the mother, but he is still responsible for making child support payments
   B. suspect that he is complaining about the mother in order to avoid his own responsibility for making child support payments
   C. are concerned with his responsibility to make child support payments, not with the mother's abuse of the child
   D. can not determine his responsibility for making child support payments until his complaint about the mother is investigated

   1.____

2. You are interviewing an elderly woman who lives alone to determine her eligibility for homemaker service at public expense. Though obviously frail and in need of this service, the woman is not completely cooperative, and during the interview, is often silent for a considerable period of time.
   Of the following, the *BEST* way for you to deal with these periods of silence is to

   A. realize that she may be embarrassed to have to apply for homemaker service at public expense, and emphasize her right to this service
   B. postpone the interview and make an appointment with her for a later date, when she may be better able to cooperate
   C. explain to the woman that you have many clients to interview and need her cooperation to complete the interview quickly
   D. recognize that she is probably hiding something and begin to ask questions to draw her out

   2.____

3. During a conference with an adolescent boy at a juvenile detention center, you find out for the first time that he would prefer to be placed in foster care rather than return to his natural parents.
   To uncover the reasons why the boy dislikes his own home, of the following, it would be *MOST* advisable for you to

   A. ask the boy a number of short, simple questions about his feelings
   B. encourage the boy to talk freely and express his feelings as best he can
   C. interview the parents and find out why the boy doesn't want to live at home
   D. administer a battery of psychological tests in order to make an assessment of the boy's problems

   3.____

4. You are interviewing a mother who is applying for Aid to Families with Dependent Children because the husband has deserted the family. The mother becomes annoyed at having to answer your questions and tells you to leave her apartment.
   Which one of the following actions would be *most appropriate* to take *FIRST* in this situation?

   4.____

A. Return to the office and close the case for lack of cooperation
B. Tell the mother that you will get the information from her neighbors if she does not cooperate
C. Tell the mother that you must stay until you get answers to your questions
D. Explain to the mother the reasons for the interview and the consequences of Her failure to cooperate

5. A counselor counseling juvenile clients finds that, although he can tolerate most of their behavior, he becomes infuriated when they lie to him.
Of the following, the counselor can BEST deal with his anger at his clients' lying by

   A. recognizing his feelings of anger and learning to control expression of these feelings to his clients
   B. warning his clients that he cannot be responsible for his anger when a client lies to him
   C. using will power to suppress his feelings of anger when a client lies to him
   D. realizing that lying is a common trait of juveniles and not directed against him personally

6. During an interview, one of your clients, a former drug addict, has expressed an interest in attending a community counseling center and resuming his education.
In this case, the MOST appropriate action that you should take FIRST is to

   A. determine whether this ambition is realistic for a former drug addict
   B. send the client's application to a community counseling center which provides services to former addicts
   C. ask the client whether he is really motivated or is just seeking your approval
   D. encourage and assist the client to take this step, since his interest is a positive sign

7. You are interviewing a client who, during previous appointments, has not responded to your requests for information required to determine his continued eligibility for services. On this occasion, the client again offers an excuse which you feel is not acceptable.
For you to advise the client of the probable loss of services because of his lack of cooperation is

   A. *inappropriate,* because the threat to withhold services will harm the relationship between counselor and client
   B. *inappropriate,* because counselors should not reveal to clients that they do not believe their statements
   C. *appropriate,* because social services are a reward given to cooperative clients
   D. *appropriate,* beca,us.e the counselor should Inform clients of the consequences of their lack of cooperation

8. Assume that you are counselling an adolescent boy in a juvenile detention center who has been a ringleader in smuggling "pot" into the center.
During your regular interview with this boy, of the following, it would be *advisable* to

   A. tell him you know that he has been involved in smuggling pot and that you are trying to understand the reasons for his misbehavior
   B. ignore his pot smuggling in order to reassure him that you understand and accept him, even though you do not agree with his standards of behavior
   C. warn him that you have reported his pot smuggling and that he will be punished for his misbehavior
   D. show him that you disapprove of his pot smuggling, but assure him that you will not report him for his misbehavior

9. Your unit has received several complaints about a homeless elderly woman living outdoors in various locations in the area. To help determine the need for protective services for this woman, you interview several persons in the neighborhood who are familiar with her, but all are uncooperative or reluctant to give information.
Of the following, your BEST approach to these persons is to explain to them that

   A. you will take legal steps against them if they do not cooperate with you
   B. their cooperation may enable you to help this homeless woman
   C. you need their cooperation to remove this homeless woman from their neighborhood
   D. they will be responsible for any harm that comes to this homeless woman

9.____

10. Assume that you are interviewing a client regarding an adjustment in budget. The client begins to scream at you that she holds you responsible for the decrease in her allowance.
Of the following, which is the BEST way for you to handle this situation?

   A. Attempt to discuss the matter calmly with the client and explain her right to a hearing
   B. Urge the client to appeal and assure her of your support
   C. Tell the client that her disorderly behavior will be held against her
   D. Tell the client that the reduction is "due to red tape" and is not your fault

10.____

11. As a counselor assigned to a juvenile detention center, you are having a counselling interview with a recently admitted boy who is having serious problems in adjusting to confinement in the center. During the interview, the boy frequently interrupts to ask you personal questions. Of the following, the BEST way for you to deal with these questions is to

   A. tell him in a friendly way that your job is to discuss his problems, not yours
   B. try to understand how the questions relate to the boy's own problems and reply with discretion
   C. take no notice of the questions and continue with the interview
   D. try to win the boy's confidence by answering his questions in detail

11.____

12. A counselor is interviewing an elderly woman who hesitates to provide necessary information about her finances to determine whether she is eligible for supplementary assistance. She fears that this information will be reported to others and that her neighbors will find out that she is destitute and applying for "welfare." Of the following, the counselor's MOST appropriate response is to

   A. tell her that, if she hesitates to give this information, the agency will get it from other sources
   B. assure her that this information is kept strictly confidential and will not be given to unauthorized persons
   C. convince her that her application will be turned down unless she provides this information as soon as possible
   D. ask for the name and address of her nearest relative and obtain the information from that person

12.____

13. You are counseling a couple whose children have been placed in a foster home because of the couple's quarreling and child neglect. When you interview the wife by herself, she tells you that she knows the husband often "cheats" on her with other women, but she is too afraid of the husband's temper to tell him how much this hurts her.
For you to immediately reveal to the husband the wife's unhappiness concerning his "cheating" is, generally,

   A. *good practice,* because it will help the husband to understand why his wife quarrels with him
   B. *poor practice,* because information received from the wife should not be given to the husband without her permission
   C. *good practice,* because the husband will direct his anger at you rather than at his wife
   D. poor *practice,* because the wife may have told you a false story about her husband in order to win your sympathy

14. A counselor is beginning a job placement interview with a tall, strongly built young man. As the man sits down, the counselor comments: "I know a big fellow like you wouldn't be interested in any clerical job."
For the counselor to make such a comment is, generally,

   A. *appropriate,* because it creates an air of familiarity which may put the man at ease
   B. *inappropriate,* because the man may be sensitive about his physical size
   C. *appropriate,* because, the counselor is using his judgment to help speed up the interview
   D. *inappropriate,* because the man may feel he is being pressured into agreeing with the counselor

15. A counselor in a men's shelter is counseling a middle-aged client for alcoholism. During counseling, the" client confesses that, many years ago, he had often enjoyed sexually abusing his ten-year-old daughter. The counselor tells the client that he personally finds the client's behavior "morally disgusting."
For the counselor to tell the client this is, generally,

   A. *acceptable counseling practice,* because it may encourage the client to feel guilty about his behavior
   B. *unacceptable couseling practice*, because the client may try to shock the counselor by confessing other similar behavior
   C. *acceptable counseling practice,* because "letting off steam" in this manner may relieve tension between the counselor and the client
   D. *unacceptable counseling practice,* because the client may hesitate to discuss his behavior frankly with the counselor in the future

16. During an interview, your client, who wants to move to a larger apartment, asks you to decide on a suitable neighborhood for her.
For you to make such a decision for the client would, generally, be considered

   A. *appropriate,* because you can save time and expense by sharing your knowledge of neighborhoods with the client
   B. *inappropriate,* because counselors should not help clients with this type of decision
   C. *appropriate,* because this will help the client to develop confidence in her ability to make decisions
   D. *inappropriate,* because the client should be encouraged to accept the responsibility of making this decision

17. A client tells you that he is extremely upset by the treatment that he received from Center personnel at the information desk.
Which of the following is the *BEST* way to handle this complaint during the interview?

   A. Explain to the client that he probably misinterpreted what occurred at the information desk
   B. Let the client express his feelings and then proceed with the interview
   C. Tell the client that you are not concerned with the personnel at the information desk
   D. Escort the client to the information desk to find out what really happened

18. You are finishing an interview with a client in which you have explained to her the procedure she must go through to apply for income maintenance.
Of the following, the *BEST* way for you to make sure that she has fully understood the procedure is to ask her

   A. whether she feels she has understood your explanation of the procedure
   B. whether she has any questions to ask you about the procedure
   C. to describe the procedure to you in her own words
   D. a few questions to test her understanding of the procedure

19. You are interviewing a client in his home as part of your investigation of an anonymous complaint that he has been receiving Medicaid fraudulently. During the interview, the client frequently interrupts your questions to discuss the hardships of his life and the bitterness he feels about his medical condition.
Of the following, the *BEST* way for you to deal with these discussions is to

   A. cut them off abruptly, since the client is probably just trying to avoid answering your questions
   B. listen patiently, since these discussions may be helpful to the client and may give you information for your investigation
   C. remind the client that you are investigating a complaint against him and he must answer directly
   D. seek to gain the client's confidence by discussing any personal or medical problems which you yourself may have

20. While interviewing an absent father to determine his ability to pay child supprt, you realize that his answers to some of your questions contradict his answers to other questions. Of the following, the *BEST* way for you to try to get accurate information from the father is to

    A. confront him with his contradictory answers and demand an explanation from him
    B. use your best judgment as to which of his answers are accurate and question him accordingly
    C. tell him that he has misunderstood your questions and that he must clarify his answers
    D. ask him the same questions in different words and follow up his answers with related questions

21. The one of the following types of interviewees who presents the *LEAST* difficult problem to handle is the person who

    A. answers with a great many qualifications
    B. talks at length about unrelated subjects so that the counselor cannot ask questions
    C. has difficulty understanding the counselor's vocabulary
    D. breaks into the middle of sentences and completes them with a meaning of his own

22. A man being interviewed is entitled to Medicaid, but he refuses to sign up for it because he says he cannot accept any form of welfare.
    Of the following, the *BEST* course of action to take *FIRST* is to

    A. try to discover the reason for his feeling this way
    B. tell him that he should be glad financial help is available
    C. explain that others cannot help him if he will not help himself
    D. suggest that he speak to someone who is already on Medicaid

23. Of the following, the outcome of an interview by a counselor depends *MOST* heavily on the

    A. personality of the interviewee
    B. personality of the counselor
    C. subject matter of the questions asked
    D. interaction between counselor and interviewee.

24. Some clients being interviewed are primarily interested in making a favorable impression. The counselor should be aware of the fact that such clients are *more likely* than other clients to

    A. try to anticipate the answers the interviewer is looking for
    B. answer all questions openly and frankly
    C. try to assume the role of interviewer
    D. be anxious to get the interview over as quickly as possible

25. The type of interview which a counselor usually conducts is substantially different from most interviewing situations in all of the following aspects *EXCEPT* the

    A. setting   B. kinds of clients
    C. techniques employed   D. kinds of problems

KEY (CORRECT ANSWERS)

1. A
2. A
3. B
4. D
5. A

6. D
7. D
8. A
9. B
10. A

11. B
12. B
13. B
14. D
15. D

16. D
17. B
18. C
19. B
20. D

21. C
22. A
23. D
24. A
25. C

EXAMINATION SECTION

TEST 1

DIRECTIONS: Each question or incomplete statement is followed by several suggested answers or completions. Select the one that BEST answers the question or completes the statement. *PRINT THE LETTER OF THE CORRECT ANSWER IN THE SPACE AT THE RIGHT.*

1. One of the major objectives of a pre-employment interview is to get the interviewee to respond freely to inquiries.
   The one of the following actions that would be MOST likely to restrict the conversation of the interviewee would be for the investigator to
   A. keep a stenographic record of the interviewee's statements
   B. ask questions requiring complete explanations
   C. pose direct, specific questions to the interviewee
   D. allow the interviewee to respond to questions at his own pace

   1.____

2. One of the reasons for the widespread use of the interview in personnel selection is that the interview
   A. has been shown to be a valid measurement technique
   B. is efficient and reliable
   C. has been demonstrated to result in consistency among raters
   D. allows for flexibility of response

   2.____

3. In conducting a personnel interview, which of the following guidelines would be MOST desirable for the interviewer to follow?
   A. Allocate the same amount of time to each person being interviewed to standardize the process
   B. Ask exactly the same questions of all persons being interviewed to increase the objectivity of the process
   C. Eliminate the use of non-directive techniques because of their subjectivity
   D. Vary his style and technique to fit the purpose of the interview and the people being interviewed

   3.____

4. You are planning to conduct preliminary interviews of applicants for an important position in your department.
   Which of the following planning considerations is LEAST likely to contribute to successful interviews?
   A. Make provisions to conduct interviews in privacy
   B. Schedule your appointments so that interviews will be short
   C. Prepare a list of your objectives
   D. Learn as much as you can about the applicant before the interview

   4.____

5. When dealing with an aggrieved worker, a USEFUL interviewing technique is to
   A. maintain a sympathetic attitude
   B. maintain an attitude of cold impartiality

   5.____

C. assure the subject that you are on his side
D. display a tape recorder to give the subject confidence that no parts of his story will be overlooked

6. The "patterned interview" is a device used by sophisticated employers to
   A. select employees who fit the ethnic pattern of the community
   B. ascertain the pattern of facts surrounding a grievance
   C. discourage workers from joining unions
   D. appraises a subject's most important character traits

6._____

7. One of the applicants for a menial job is a tall, stooped, husky individual with a low forehead, narrow eyes, a protruding chin, and a tendency to keep his mouth open.
   In interviewing him, you should
   A. check him more carefully than the other applicants regarding criminal background
   B. disregard any skills he might have for other jobs which are vacant
   C. make your vocabulary somewhat simpler than with the other applicants
   D. make no assumptions regarding his ability on the basis of his appearance

7._____

8. Of the following, the BEST approach for you to use at the beginning of an interview with a job applicant is to
   A. caution him to use his time economically and to get to the point
   B. ask him how long he intends to remain on the job if hired
   C. make some pleasant remarks to put him at ease
   D. emphasize the importance of the interview in obtaining the job

8._____

9. Of the following, the BEST reason for conducting an "exit interview" with an employee is to
   A. make certain that he returns all identification cards and office keys
   B. find out why he is leaving
   C. provide a useful training device for the exit interviewer
   D. discover if his initial hiring was in error

9._____

10. If you are to interview several applicants for jobs and rate them on five different factors on a scale of 1 to 5, you should be MOST careful to *insure* that your
    A. rating on one factor does not influence your rating on another factor
    B. ratings on all factors are interrelated with a minimum of variation
    C. overall evaluation for employment exactly reflects the arithmetic average of your ratings
    D. overall evaluation for employment is unrelated to your individual ratings

10._____

11. Of the following, the question MOST appropriate for initial screening purposes GENERALLY is:
    A. What are your salary requirements?
    B. Why do you think you would like this kind of work?
    C. How did you get along with your last supervisor?
    D. What are your vocational goals?

11._____

12. Of the following, normally the question MOST appropriate for selection purposes generally would tend to be:
    A. Where did you work last?
    B. When did you graduate from high school?
    C. What was your average in school?
    D. Why did you select this organization?

12.____

13. Assume that you have been asked to interview each of several students who have been hired to work part-time.
    Which of the following would ordinarily be accomplished LEAST effectively in such an interview?
    A. Providing information about the organization or institution in which the students will be working
    B. Directing the students to report for work each afternoon at specified times
    C. Determining experience and background of the students so that appropriate assignments can be made
    D. Changing the attitudes of the students toward the importance of parental controls

13.____

14. In interviewing job applicants, which of the following usually does NOT have to be done before the end of the interview?
    A. Making a decision to hire an applicant
    B. Securing information from applicants
    C. Giving information to applicants
    D. Establishing a friendly relationship with applicants

14.____

15. In the process of interviewing applicants for a position on your staff, the one of the following which would be BEST is to
    A. make sure all applicants are introduced to the other members of your staff prior to the formal interview
    B. make sure the applicant does not ask questions about the job or the department
    C. avoid having the applicant talk with the staff at the conclusion of a successful interview
    D. introduce applicants to some of the staff at the conclusion of a successful interview

15.____

16. While interviewing a job applicant, you ask applicant why he left his last job. The applicant does not answer immediately.
    Of the following, the BEST action to take at that point is to
    A. wait until he answers
    B. ask another question
    C. repeat the question in a loud voice
    D. ask him why he does not answer

16.____

17. You know that a student applying for a job in your office has done well in college except for two courses in science. However, when you ask him about his grades, his reply is vague and general.

17.____

It would be BEST for you to
- A. lead the applicant to admitting doing poorly in science to be sure that the facts are correct
- B. judge the applicant's tact and skill in handling what may be for him a personally sensitive question
- C. immediately confront the applicant with the facts and ask for an explanation
- D. ignore the applicant's response since you have the transcript

18. A college student has applied for a position with your department. Prior to conducting an interview of the job applicant, it would be LEAST helpful for you to have
    - A. a personal resume
    - B. a job description
    - C. references
    - D. hiring requirements

19. Job applicants tend to be nervous during interviews. Which of the following techniques is MOST likely to put such an applicant at ease?
    - A. Try to establish rapport by asking general questions which are easily answered by the applicant
    - B. Ask the applicant to describe his career objectives immediately, thus minimizing the anxiety caused by waiting
    - C. Start the interview with another member of the staff present so that the applicant does not feel alone
    - D. Proceed as rapidly as possible, since the emotional state of the applicant is none of your concern

20. At the first interview between a supervisor and a newly appointed subordinate, GREATEST care should be taken to
    - A. build toward a satisfactory personal relationship even if some other objectives of the interview must be postponed
    - B. cover a predetermined list of specific objectives so as to make a further orientation interview unnecessary
    - C. create an image of a forceful, determined supervisor whose wishes cannot be opposed by a subordinate without great risk
    - D. create an impression of efficiency and control of operation free from interpersonal relationships

21. You are a supervisor in an agency and are holding your first interview with a new employee.
    In this interview, you should strive MAINLY to
    - A. show the new employee that you are an efficient and objective supervisor, with a completely impersonal attitude toward your subordinates
    - B. complete the entire orientation process including the giving of detailed job-duty instructions

C. make it clear to the employee that all your decisions are based on your many years of experience
D. lay the groundwork for a good employee-supervisor relationship by gaining the new employee's confidence

22. The INCORRECT statement related to the principles of interviewing is:
    A. Written outlines should be avoided by the interviewer because they tend to be overly restrictive.
    B. Preliminary planning (for the interview) should involve an analysis of the point of view of the person to be interviewed.
    C. An interviewing supervisor should make every effort to conduct it in privacy to avoid possible inhibitions.
    D. Well-planned questions are sometimes necessary in conducting an interview.

23. Assume that you are conducting an interview with a prospective employee who is of limited mental ability and low socio-economic status.
    Of the following, it is MOST likely that asking him many open-ended questions about his work experience would cause him to respond
    A. articulately   B. reluctantly   C. comfortably   D. aggressively

24. An individual interview is to be used as part of an examination for a supervisory position.
    Of the following, the attribute or characteristic that is LEAST suitable for evaluation in such an interview is
    A. ability to supervise people   B. poise and confidence
    C. response to stress conditions   D. rigidity and flexibility

25. In conducting a disciplinary interview, a supervisor finds that he must ask some highly personal questions which are relevant to the problem at hand.
    The interviewer is MOST likely to get TRUTHFUL answers to these questions if he asks them
    A. early in the interview, before the interviewee has had a chance to become emotional
    B. in a manner so that the interviewee can answer them with a simple "yes" or "no"
    C. well into the interview, after rapport and trust have been established
    D. just after the close of the interview, so that the questions appear to be off the record

KEY (CORRECT ANSWERS)

1. A
2. D
3. D
4. B
5. A

6. D
7. D
8. C
9. B
10. A

11. A
12. D
13. D
14. A
15. D

16. A
17. B
18. C
19. A
20. A

21. D
22. A
23. B
24. A
25. C

TEST 2

DIRECTIONS: Each question or incomplete statement is followed by several suggested answers or completions. Select the one that BEST answers the question or completes the statement. *PRINT THE LETTER OF THE CORRECT ANSWER IN THE SPACE AT THE RIGHT.*

1. Of the following methods of conducting an interview, the BEST is to
   A. ask questions with "yes" or "no" answers
   B. listen carefully and ask only questions that are pertinent
   C. fire questions at the interviewee so that he must answer sincerely and briefly
   D. read standardized questions to the person being interviewed

   1.____

2. An interviewer should begin with topics which are easy to talk about and which are not threatening.
   This procedure is useful MAINLY because it
   A. allows the applicant a little time to get accustomed to the situation and leads to freer communication
   B. distracts the attention of the person being interviewed from the main purpose of the questioning
   C. is the best way for the interviewer to show that he is relaxed and confident on the job
   D. causes the interviewee to feel that the interviewer is apportioning valuable questioning time

   2.____

3. The initial interview will normally be more of a problem to the interviewer than any subsequent interviews he may have with the same person because
   A. the interviewee is likely to be hostile
   B. there is too much to be accomplished in one session
   C. he has less information about the client than he will have later
   D. some information may be forgotten when later making record of this first interview

   3.____

4. Most successful interviews are those in which the interviewer shows a genuine interest in the person he is questioning.
   This attitude would MOST likely cause the individual being interviewed to
   A. feel that the interviewer already knows all the facts in his case
   B. act more naturally and reveal more of his true feelings
   C. request that the interviewer give more attention to his problems, not his personality
   D. react defensively, suppress his negative feelings and conceal the real facts in his case

   4.____

5. When interviewing a person, the interviewer may easily slip into error in rating his subject's personal qualities because of the general impression he receives of the individual.
   This tendency is known as the
   A. "halo" effect
   B. subjective bias problem
   C. "person-to-person" error
   D. inflation effect

   5.____

6. An interviewer would find an interview checklist LEAST useful for 6.____
   A. making sure that all the principal facts are secured in the interview
   B. insuring that the claimant's grievance is settled in his favor
   C. facilitating later research into the nature of the problems handled by the agency
   D. conducting the interview in a logical and orderly fashion

7. There are almost as many techniques of interviewing as there are interviews. Of the following, the LEAST objectionable method is to 7.____
   A. ask if interviewee minds being quoted
   B. make occasional notes as important topics some up
   C. take notes unobtrusively
   D. take shorthand notes of every word

8. Questions worded so that the person being interviewed has some hint of the desired answer can modify the person's response. 8.____
   The result of the inclusion of such questions in an interview, even when they ae used inadvertently, is to
   A. have no effect on the basic content of the information given by the person interviewed
   B. have value in convincing the person that the suggested plan is the best for him
   C. cause the person to give more meaningful information
   D. reduce the validity of the meaningful information obtained from the person

9. The person MOST likely to be a good interviewer is one who 9.____
   A. is able to outguess the person being interviewed
   B. tries to change the attitudes of the persons he interviews
   C. controls the interview by skillfully dominating the conversation
   D. is able to imagine himself in the position of the person being interviewed

10. The "halo effect" is an overall impression on the interviewee, whether favorable or unfavorable, usually created by a single trait. This impression then influences the appraisal of all other factors. 10.____
    A "halo effect" is LEAST likely to be created at an interview where the interviewee is a
    A. person of average appearance and ability
    B. rough-looking man who uses abusive language
    C. young attractive woman being interviewed by a man
    D. person who demonstrates an exceptional ability to remember faces

11. Of the following, the BEST way for an interviewer to calm a person who seems to have become emotionally upset as a result of a question asked is for the interviewer to 11.____
    A. talk to the person about other things for a short time
    B. ask that the person control himself
    C. probe for the cause of his emotional upset
    D. finish the questioning as quickly as possible

12. Of the following, the GREATEST pitfall in interviewing is that the result may be affected by the
    A. bias of the interviewee
    B. bias of the interviewer
    C. educational level of the interviewee
    D. educational level of the interviewer

13. Assume you are assigned to interview applicants.
    Of the following, which is the BEST attitude for you to take in dealing with applicants?
    A. Assume they will enjoy being interviewed because they believe that you have the power of decision
    B. Expect that they have a history of anti-social behavior in the family, and probe deeply into the social development of family members
    C. Expect that they will try to control the interview, thus you should keep them on the defensive
    D. Assume that they will be polite and cooperative and attempt to secure the information you need in a business-like manner

14. A Spanish-speaking applicant may want to bring his bilingual child with him to an interview to act as an interpreter.
    Which of the following would be LEAST likely to affect the value of an interview in which an applicant's child has acted as interpreter?
    A. It may make it undesirable to ask certain questions.
    B. A child may do an inadequate job of interpretation.
    C. A child's answers may indicate his feelings toward his parents.
    D. The applicant may not want to reveal all information in front of his child.

15. In answering questions asked by students, faculty, and the public, it is MOST important that
    A. you indicate your source of information
    B. you are not held responsible for the answers
    C. the facts you give be accurate
    D. the answers cover every possible aspect of each question

16. Assume that someone you are interviewing is reluctant to give you certain information.
    He would probably be MORE responsive if you show him that
    A. all the other persons you interviewed provided you with the information
    B. it would serve his own best interests to give you the information
    C. the information is very important to you
    D. you are business-like and take a no-nonsense approach

17. Taking notes while you are interviewing someone is MOST likely to
    A. arouse doubts as to your trustworthiness
    B. give the interviewee confidence in your ability
    C. insure that you record the facts you think are important
    D. make the responses of the interviewee unreliable

18. In developing a role-playing situation to be used to train interviewers, the one of the following that it would be MOST important to use as a guide is that the situation
    A. allow the role player to identify readily with the role he is to play
    B. be free of actual or potential conflict between the role players
    C. can be clearly recognized by the participants as an actual interview situation that has already taken place
    D. should provide a detailed set of specifications for handling the roles to be played

19. Restating a question before the person being interviewed gives an answer to the original question is usually NOT good practice principally because
    A. the client will think that you don't know your job
    B. it may confuse the client
    C. the interviewer should know exactly what to ask and how to put the question
    D. it reveals the interviewer's insecurity

20. In interviewing a man who has a grievance, it is IMPORTANT that the interviewer
    A. take note of such physical responses as shifty eyes
    B. use a lie detector, if possible, to ascertain the truth in doubtful situations
    C. allow the complainant to "tell his story"
    D. place the complainant under oath

21. Ideally, the setting for an interview should NOT include
    A. an informal opening
    B. privacy and comfort
    C. an atmosphere of leisure
    D. a lie detector

22. Which of the following is an example of a "non-directive" interview?
    A. The subject directs his remarks at someone other than the interviewer.
    B. The subject discusses any topics that seem to be relevant to him.
    C. The subject has not been directed that he need answer any particular questions.
    D. The interview is confined to the facts of the case and is not directed at eliciting personal information.

23. Of the following abilities, the one which is LEAST important in conducting an interview is the ability to
    A. ask the interviewee pertinent questions
    B. evaluate the interviewee on the basis of appearance
    C. evaluate the responses of the interviewee
    D. gain the cooperation of the interviewee

24. Which of the following actions would be LEAST desirable for you to take when you have to conduct an interview?
    A. Set a relaxed and friendly atmosphere
    B. Plan your interview ahead of time
    C. Allow the person interviewed to structure the interview as he wishes
    D. Include some stock or standard question which you ask everyone.

    24._____

25. One of the MOST important techniques for conducting good interviews is
    A. asking the applicant questions in rapid succession, thereby keeping the conversation properly focused
    B. listening carefully to all that the applicant has to say, making mental notes of possible areas for follow-up
    C. indicating to the applicant the criteria and standards on which you will base your judgment
    D. making sure that you are interrupted about five minutes before you wish to end so that you can keep on schedule

    25._____

KEY (CORRECT ANSWERS)

1.	B		11.	A
2.	A		12.	B
3.	C		13.	D
4.	B		14.	C
5.	A		15.	C
6.	B		16.	B
7.	C		17.	C
8.	D		18.	A
9.	D		19.	B
10.	A		20.	C

21. D
22. B
23. B
24. C
25. B

PREPARING WRITTEN MATERIAL

EXAMINATION SECTION

TEST 1

DIRECTIONS: Each of the sentences in this test may be classified under one of the following four categories:
  A. *Incorrect* because of faulty grammar or sentence structure
  B. *Incorrect* because of faulty punctuation
  C. *Incorrect* because of faulty capitalization
  D. *Correct*

Examine each sentence carefully to determine under which of the above four options it is best classified. Then, in the space at the right, print the capital letter preceding the option which is the BEST of the four suggested above.

(Each incorrect sentence contains but one type of error. Consider a sentence to be correct if it contains none of the types of errors mentioned, even though there may be other correct ways of expressing the same thought.)

1. This fact, together with those brought out at the previous meeting, prove that the schedule is satisfactory to the employees.   1.____

2. Like many employees in scientific fields, the work of bookkeepers and accountants requires accuracy and neatness.   2.____

3. "What can I do for you," the secretary asked as she motioned to the visitor to take a seat.   3.____

4. Our representative, Mr. Charles will call on you next week to determine whether or not your claim has merit.   4.____

5. We expect you to return in the spring; please do not disappoint us.   5.____

6. Any supervisor, who disregards the just complaints of his subordinates, is remiss in the performance of his duty.   6.____

7. Because she took less than an hour for lunch is no reason for permitting her to leave before five o'clock.   7.____

8. "Miss Smith," said the supervisor, "Please arrange a meeting of the staff for two o'clock on Monday."   8.____

9. A private company's vacation and sick leave allowance usually differs considerably from a public agency.   9.____

10. Therefore, in order to increase the efficiency of operations in the department, a report on the recommended changes in procedures was presented to the departmental committee in charge of the program.   10.____

149

11. We told him to assign the work to whoever was available.   11._____

12. Since John was the most efficient of any other employee in the bureau, he received the highest service rating.   12._____

13. Only those members of the national organization who resided in the middle West attended the conference in Chicago.   13._____

14. The question of whether the office manager has as yet attained, or indeed can ever hope to secure professional status is one which has been discussed for years.   14._____

15. No one knew who to blame for the error which, we later discovered, resulted in a considerable loss of time.   15._____

KEY (CORRECT ANSWERS)

1.	A	6.	B	11.	D
2.	A	7.	A	12.	A
3.	B	8.	C	13.	C
4.	B	9.	A	14.	B
5.	D	10.	D	15.	A

TEST 2

DIRECTIONS: Each of the sentences in this test may be classified under one of the following four categories:
- A. *Incorrect* because of faulty grammar or sentence structure
- B. *Incorrect* because of faulty punctuation
- C. *Incorrect* because of faulty capitalization
- D. *Correct*

1. The National alliance of Businessmen is trying to persuade private businesses to hire youth in the summertime. 1.____

2. The supervisor who is on vacation, is in charge of processing vouchers. 2.____

3. The activity of the committee at its conferences is always stimulating. 3.____

4. After checking the addresses again, the letters went to the mailroom. 4.____

5. The director, as well as the employees, are interested in sharing the dividends. 5.____

KEY (CORRECT ANSWERS)

1. C
2. B
3. D
4. A
5. A

TEST 3

DIRECTIONS: In each of the following groups of sentences, one of the four sentences is faulty in grammar, punctuation, or capitalization. Select the INCORRECT sentence in each case.

1. A. Sailing down the bay was a thrilling experience for me.
   B. He was not consulted about your joining the club.
   C. This story is different than the one I told you yesterday.
   D. There is no doubt about his being the best player.

2. A. He maintains there is but one road to world peace.
   B. It is common knowledge that a child sees much he is not supposed to see.
   C. Much of the bitterness might have been avoided if arbitration had been resorted to earlier in the meeting.
   D. The man decided it would be advisable to marry a girl somewhat younger than him.

3. A. In this book, the incident I liked least is where the hero tries to put out the forest fire.
   B. Learning a foreign language will undoubtedly give a person a better understanding of his mother tongue.
   C. His actions made us wonder what he planned to do next.
   D. Because of the war, we were unable to travel during the summer vacation.

4. A. The class had no sooner become interested in the lesson than the dismissal bell rang.
   B. There is little agreement about the kind of world to be planned at the peace conference.
   C. "Today," said the teacher, "we shall read 'The Wind in the Willows,' I am sure you'll like it.
   D. The terms of the legal settlement of the family quarrel handicapped both sides for many years.

5. A. I was so surprised that I was not able to say a word.
   B. She is taller than any other member of the class.
   C. It would be much more preferable if you were never seen in his company.
   D. We had no choice but to excuse her for being late.

KEY (CORRECT ANSWERS)

1. C
2. D
3. A
4. C
5. C

TEST 4

DIRECTIONS: In each of the following groups of sentences, one of the four sentences is faulty in grammar, punctuation, or capitalization. Select the INCORRECT sentence in each case.

1. A. Please send me these data at the earliest opportunity.
   B. The loss of their material proved to be a severe handicap.
   C. My principal objection to this plan is that it is impracticable.
   D. The doll had laid in the rain for an hour and was ruined.

2. A. The garden scissors, left out all night in the rain, were in a badly rusted condition.
   B. The girls felt bad about the misunderstanding which had arisen
   C. Sitting near the campfire, the old man told John and I about many exciting adventures he had had.
   D. Neither of us is in a position to undertake a task of that magnitude.

3. A. The general concluded that one of the three roads would lead to the besieged city.
   B. The children didn't, as a rule, do hardly anything beyond what they were told to do.
   C. The reason the girl gave for her negligence was that she had acted on the spur of the moment.
   D. The daffodils and tulips look beautiful in that blue vase.

4. A. If I was ten years older, I should be interested in this work.
   B. Give the prize to whoever has drawn the best picture.
   C. When you have finished reading the book, take it back to the library.
   D. My drawing is as good as or better than yours.

5. A. He asked me whether the substance was animal or vegetable.
   B. An apple which is unripe should not be eaten by a child.
   C. That was an insult to me who am your friend.
   D. Some spy must of reported the matter to the enemy.

6. A. Limited time makes quoting the entire message impossible.
   B. Who did she say was going?
   C. The girls in your class have dressed more dolls this year than we.
   D. There was such a large amount of books on the floor that I couldn't find a place for my rocking chair.

7. A. What with his sleeplessness and his ill health, he was unable to assume any responsibility for the success of the meeting.
   B. If I had been born in February, I should be celebrating my birthday soon.
   C. In order to prevent breakage, she placed a sheet of paper between each of the plates when she packed them.
   D. After the spring shower, the violets smelled very sweet.

1.____
2.____
3.____
4.____
5.____
6.____
7.____

2 (#4)

8. A. He had laid the book down very reluctantly before the end of the lesson.   8.____
    B. The dog, I am sorry to say, had lain on the bed all night.
    C. The cloth was first lain on a flat surface; then it was pressed with a hot iron.
    D. While we were in Florida, we lay in the sun until we were noticeably tanned.

9. A. If John was in New York during the recent holiday season, I have no doubt   9.____
       he spent most of the time with his parents.
    B. How could he enjoy the television program; the dog was barking and the
       baby was crying.
    C. When the problem was explained to the class, he must have been asleep.
    D. She wished that her new dress were finished so that she could go to the
       party.

10. A. The engine not only furnishes power but light and heat as well.   10.____
    B. You're aware that we've forgotten whose guilt was established, aren't you?
    C. Everybody knows that the woman made many sacrifices for her children.
    D. A man with his dog and gun is a familiar sight in this neighborhood.

KEY (CORRECT ANSWERS)

1.	D	6.	D
2.	C	7.	B
3.	B	8.	C
4.	A	9.	B
5.	D	10.	A

TEST 5

DIRECTIONS: Each of Questions 1 through 5 consists of a sentence which may be classified appropriately under one of the following four categories:
- A. *Incorrect* because of faulty grammar
- B. *Incorrect* because of faulty punctuation
- C. *Incorrect* because of faulty spelling
- D. *Correct*

Examine each sentence carefully. Then, print in the space at the right the letter preceding the category which is the BEST of the four suggested above

(Note: Each incorrect sentence contains only one type of error. Consider a sentence correct if it contains no errors, although there may be other correct ways of writing the sentence.)

1. Of the two employees, the one in our office is the most efficient.   1.____

2. No one can apply or even understand, the new rules and regulations.   2.____

3. A large amount of supplies were stored in the empty office.   3.____

4. If an employee is occassionally asked to work overtime, he should do so willingly.   4.____

5. It is true that the new procedures are difficult to use but, we are certain that you will learn them quickly.   5.____

6. The office manager said that he did not know who would be given a large allotment under the new plan.   6.____

7. It was at the supervisor's request that the clerk agreed to postpone his vacation.   7.____

8. We do not believe that it is necessary for both he and the clerk to attend the conference.   8.____

9. All employees, who display perseverance, will be given adequate recognition.   9.____

10. He regrets that some of us employees are dissatisfied with our new assignments.   10.____

11. "Do you think that the raise was merited," asked the supervisor?   11.____

12. The new manual of procedure is a valuable supplament to our rules and regulations.   12.____

13. The typist admitted that she had attempted to pursuade the other employees to assist her in her work.   13.____

2 (#5)

14. The supervisor asked that all amendments to the regulations be handled by you and I. 14._____

15. The custodian seen the boy who broke the window. 15._____

KEY (CORRECT ANSWERS)

1.	A	6.	D	11.	B
2.	B	7.	D	12.	C
3.	A	8.	A	13.	C
4.	C	9.	B	14.	A
5.	B	10.	D	15.	A

PREPARING WRITTEN MATERIAL

PARAGRAPH REARRANGEMENT
COMMENTARY

The sentences that follow are in scrambled order. You are to rearrange them in proper order and indicate the letter choice containing the correct answer at the space at the right.

Each group of sentences in this section is actually a paragraph presented in scrambled order. Each sentence in the group has a place in that paragraph; no sentence is to be left out. You are to read each group of sentences and decide upon the best order in which to put the sentences so as to form a well-organized paragraph.

The questions in this section measure the ability to solve a problem when all the facts relevant to its solution are not given.

More specifically, certain positions of responsibility and authority require the employee to discover connection between events sometimes, apparently, unrelated. In order to do this, the employee will find it necessary to correctly infer that unspecified events have probably occurred or are likely to occur. This ability becomes especially important when action must be taken on incomplete information.

Accordingly, these questions require competitors to choose among several suggested alternatives, each of which presents a different sequential arrangement of the events. Competitors must choose the MOST logical of the suggested sequences.

In order to do so, they may be required to draw on general knowledge to infer missing concepts or events that are essential to sequencing the given events. Competitors should be careful to infer only what is essential to the sequence. The plausibility of the wrong alternatives will always require the inclusion of unlikely events or of additional chains of events which are NOT essential to sequencing the given events.

It's very important to remember that you are looking for the best of the four possible choices, and that the best choice of all may not even be one of the answers you're given to choose from.

There is no one right way to solve these problems. Many people have found it helpful to first write out the order of the sentences, as they would have arranged them, on their scrap paper before looking at the possible answers. If their optimum answer is there, this can save them some time. If it isn't, this method can still give insight into solving the problem. Others find it most helpful to just go through each of the possible choices, contrasting each as they go along. You should use whatever method feels comfortable and works for you.

While most of these types of questions are not that difficult, we've added a higher percentage of the difficult type, just to give you more practice. Usually there are only one or two questions on this section that contain such subtle distinctions that you're unable to answer confidently. And you then may find yourself stuck deciding between two possible choices, neither of which you're sure about.

EXAMINATION SECTION

TEST 1

DIRECTIONS: The following groups of sentences need to be arranged in an order that makes sense. Select the letter preceding the sequence that represents the BEST sentence order. *PRINT THE LETTER OF THE CORRECT ANSWER IN THE SPACE AT THE RIGHT.*

1.
   I. The keyboard was purposely designed to be a little awkward to slow typists down.
   II. The arrangement of letters on the keyboard of a typewriter was not designed for the convenience of the typist.
   III. Fortunately, no one is suggesting that a new keyboard be designed right away.
   IV. If one were, we would have to learn to type all over again.
   V. The reason was that the early machines were slower than the typists and would jam easily.
   The CORRECT answer is:
   A. I, III, IV, II, V
   B. II, V, I, IV, III
   C. V, I, II, III, IV
   D. II, I, V, III, IV

   1.____

2.
   I. The majority of the new service jobs are part-time or low-paying.
   II. According to the U.S. Bureau of Labor Statistics, jobs in the service sector constitute 72% of all jobs in this country.
   III. If more and more workers receive less and less money, who will buy the goods and services needed to keep the economy going?
   IV. The service sector is by far the fastest growing part of the United States economy.
   V. Some economists look upon this trend with great concern.
   The CORRECT answer is:
   A. II, IV, I, V, III
   B. II, III, IV, I, V
   C. V, IV, II, III, I
   D. III, I, II, IV, V

   2.____

3.
   I. They can also affect one's endurance.
   II. This can stabilize blood sugar levels, and ensure that the brain is receiving a steady, constant, supply of glucose, so that one is *hitting on all cylinders* while taking the test.
   III. By food, we mean real food, not junk food or unhealthy snacks.
   IV. For this reason, it is important not to skip a meal, and to bring food with you to the exam.
   V. One's blood sugar levels can affect how clearly one is able to think and concentrate during an exam.
   The CORRECT answer is:
   A. V, IV, II, III, I
   B. V, II, I, IV, III
   C. V, I, IV, III, II
   D. V, IV, I, III, II

   3.____

4. I. Those who are the embodiment of desire are absorbed in material quests, and those who are the embodiment of feeling are warriors who value power more than possession.
    II. These qualities are in everyone, but in different degrees.
    III. But those who value understanding yearn not for goods or victory, but for knowledge.
    IV. According to Plato, human behavior flows from three main sources: desire, emotion, and knowledge.
    V. In the perfect state, the industrial forces would produce but not rule, the military would protect but not rule, and the forces of knowledge, the philosopher kings, would reign.
    The CORRECT answer is:
    A. IV, V, I, II, III
    B. V, I, II, III, IV
    C. IV, III, II, I, V
    D. IV, II, I, III, V

5. I. Of the more than 26,000 tons of garbage produced daily in New York City, 12,000 tons arrive daily at Fresh Kills.
    II. In a month, enough garbage accumulates there to fill the Empire State Building.
    III. In 1937, the Supreme Court halted the practice of dumping the trash of New York City into the sea.
    IV. Although the garbage is compacted, in a few years the mounds of garbage at Fresh Kills will be the highest points south of Maine's Mount Desert Island on the Eastern Seaboard.
    V. Instead, tugboats now pull barges of much of the trash to Staten Island and the largest landfill in the world, Fresh Kills.
    The CORRECT answer is:
    A. III, V, IV, I, II
    B. III, V, II, IV, I
    C. III, V, I, II, IV
    D. III, II, V, IV, I

6. I. Communists rank equality very high, but freedom very low.
    II. Unlike communists, conservatives place a high value on freedom and a very low value on equality.
    III. A recent study demonstrated that one way to classify people's political beliefs is to look at the importance placed on two words: freedom and equality.
    IV. Thus, by demonstrating how members of these groups feel about the two words, the study has proved to be useful for political analysts in several European countries.
    V. According to the study, socialists and liberals rank both freedom and equality very high, while fascists rate both very low.
    The CORRECT answer is:
    A. III, V, I, II, IV
    B. V, IV, III, I, II
    C. III, V, IV, II, I
    D. III, I, II, IV, V

7. I. "Can there be anything more amazing than this?"
    II. If the riddle is successfully answered, his dead brothers will be brought back to life.
    III. "Even though man sees those around him dying every day," says Dharmaraj, "he still believes and acts as if he were immortal."
    IV. "What is the cause of ceaseless wonder?" asks the Lord of the Lake.
    V. In the ancient epic, The Mahabharata, a riddle is asked of one of the Pandava brothers.
    The CORRECT answer is:
    A. V, II, I, IV, III
    B. V, IV, III, I, II
    C. V, II, IV, III, I
    D. V, II, IV, I, III

8. I. On the contrary, the two main theories—the cooperative (neoclassical) theory and the radical (labor theory)—clearly rest on very different assumptions, which have very different ethical overtones.
    II. The distribution of income is the primary factor in determining the relative levels of material well-being that different groups or individuals attain.
    III. Of all issues in economics, the distribution of income is one of the most controversial.
    IV. The neoclassical theory tends to support the existing income distribution (or minor changes), while the labor theory ends to support substantial changes in the way income is distributed.
    V. The intensity of the controversy reflects the fact that different economic theories are not purely neutral, *detached* theories with no ethical or moral implications.
    The CORRECT answer is:
    A. II, I, V, IV, III
    B. III, II, V, I, IV
    C. III, V, II, I, IV
    D. III, V, IV, I, II

9. I. The pool acts as a broker and ensures that the cheapest power gets used first.
    II. Every six seconds, the pool's computer monitors all of the generating stations in the state and decides which to ask for more power and which to cut back.
    III. The buying and selling of electrical power is handled by the New York Power Pool in Guilderland, New York.
    IV. This is to the advantage of both the buying and selling utilities.
    V. The pool began operation in 1970, and consists of the state's eight electric utilities.
    The CORRECT answer is:
    A. V, I, II, III, IV
    B. IV, II, I, III, V
    C. III, V, I, IV, II
    D. V, III, IV, II, I

10. I. Modern English is much simpler grammatically than Old English.
    II. Finnish grammar is very complicated; there are some fifteen cases, for example.
    III. Chinese, a very old language, may seem to be the exception, but it is the great number of characters/words that must be mastered that makes it so difficult to learn, not its grammar.
    IV. The newest literary language—that is, written as well as spoken—is Finish, whose literary roots go back only to about the middle of the nineteenth century.
    V. Contrary to popular belief, the longer a language is been in use the simpler its grammar—not the reverse.
    The CORRECT answer is:
    A. IV, I, II, III, V
    B. V, I, IV, II, III
    C. I, II, IV, III, V
    D. IV, II, III, I, V

10.____

KEY (CORRECT ANSWERS)

1. D 6. A
2. A 7. C
3. C 8. B
4. D 9. C
5. C 10. B

TEST 2

DIRECTIONS: This type of question tests your ability to recognize accurate paraphrasing, well-constructed paragraphs, and appropriate style and tone. It is important that the answer you select contains only the facts or concepts given in the original sentences. It is also important that you be aware of incomplete sentences, inappropriate transitions, unsupported opinions, incorrect usage, and illogical sentence order. Paragraphs that do not include all the necessary facts and concepts, that distort them, or that add new ones are not considered correct.

The format for this section may vary. Sometimes, long paragraphs are given, and emphasis is placed on style and organization. Our first five questions are of this type. Other times, the paragraphs are shorter, and there is less emphasis on style and more emphasis on accurate representation of information. Our second group of five questions are of this nature.

For each of Questions 1 through 10, select the paragraph that BEST expresses the ideas contained in the sentences above it. *PRINT THE LETTER OF THE CORRECT ANSWER IN THE SPACE AT THE RIGHT.*

1.
   I. Listening skills are very important for managers.
   II. Listening skills are not usually emphasized.
   III. Whenever managers are depicted in books, manuals or the media, they are always talking, never listening.
   IV. We'd like you to read the enclosed handout on listening skills and to try to consciously apply them this week.
   V. We guarantee they will improve the quality of your interactions.

   A. Unfortunately, listening skills are not usually emphasized for managers. Managers are always depicted as talking, never listening. We'd like you to read the enclosed handout on listening skills. Please try to apply these principles this week. If you do, we guarantee they will improve the quality of your interactions.
   B. The enclosed handout on listening skills will be important improving the quality of your interactions. We guarantee it. All you have to do is take sometime this week to read and to consciously try to apply the principles. Listening skills are very important for manages, but they are not usually emphasized. Whenever managers are depicted in books, manuals or the media, they are always talking, never listening.
   C. Listening well is one of the most important skills a manager can have, yet it's not usually given much attention. Think about any representation of managers in books, manuals, or in the media that you may have seen. They're always talking, never listening. We'd like you to read the enclosed handout on listening skills and consciously try to apply them the rest of the week. We guarantee you will see a difference in the quality of your interactions.

1.____

D. Effective listening, one very important tool in the effective manager's arsenal, is usually not emphasized enough. The usual depiction of managers in books, manuals or the media is one in which they are always talking, never listening. We'd like you to read the enclosed handout and consciously try to apply the information contained therein throughout the rest of the week. We feel sure that you will see a marked difference in the quality of your interactions.

2.
I. Chekhov wrote three dramatic masterpieces which share certain themes and formats: Uncle Vanya, The Cherry Orchard, and The Three Sisters.
II. They are primarily concerned with the passage of time and how this erodes human aspirations.
III. The plays are haunted by the ghosts of the wasted life.
IV. The characters are concerned with life's lesser problems; however, such as the inability to make decisions, loyalty to the wrong cause, and the inability to be clear.
V. This results in sweet, almost aching, type of a sadness referred to as Chekhovian.

2.____

A. Chekhov wrote three dramatic masterpieces: Uncle Vanya, The Cherry Orchard, and The Three Sisters. These masterpieces share certain themes and formats: the passage of time, how time erodes human aspirations, and the ghosts of wasted life. Each masterpiece is characterized by a sweet, almost aching, type of sadness that has become known as Chekhovian. The sweetness of this sadness hinges on the fact that it is not the great tragedies of life which are destroying these characters, but their minor flaws: indecisiveness, misplaced loyalty, unclarity.
B. The Cherry Orchard, Uncle Vanya, and The Three Sisters are three dramatic masterpieces written by Chekhov that use similar formats to explore a common theme. Each is primarily concerned with the way that passing time wears down human aspirations, and each is haunted by the ghosts of the wasted life. The characters are shown struggling futilely with the lesser problems of life: indecisiveness, loyalty to the wrong cause, and the inability to be clear. These struggles create a mood of sweet, almost aching, sadness that has become known as Chekhovian.
C. Chekhov's dramatic masterpieces are, along with The Cherry Orchard, Uncle Vanya, and The Three Sisters. These plays share certain thematic and formal similarities. They are concerned most of all with the passage of time and the way in which time erodes human aspirations. Each play is haunted by the specter of the wasted life. Chekhov's characters are caught, however, by life's lesser snares: indecisiveness, loyalty to the wrong cause, and unclarity. The characteristic mood is a sweet, almost aching type of sadness that has come to be known as Chekhovian.
D. A Chekhovian mood is characterized by sweet, almost aching, sadness. The term comes from three dramatic tragedies by Chekhov which revolve around the sadness of a wasted life. The three masterpieces (Uncle Vanya, The Three Sisters, and The Cherry Orchard) share the same

theme and format. The plays are concerned with how the passage of time erodes human aspirations. They are peopled with characters who are struggling with life's lesser problems. These are people who are indecisive, loyal to the wrong causes, or are unable to make themselves clear.

3.
I. Movie previews have often helped producers decide which parts of movies they should take out or leave in.
II. The first 1933 preview of King Kong was very helpful to the producers because many people ran screaming from the theater and would not return when four men first attacked by Kong were eaten by giant spiders.
III. The 1950 premiere of Sunset Boulevard resulted in the filming of an entirely new beginning, and a delay of six months in the film's release.
IV. In the original opening scene, William Holden was in a morgue talking with thirty-six other "corpses" about the ways some of them had died.
V. When he began to tell them of his life with Gloria Swanson, the audience found this hilarious, instead of taking the scene seriously.

3.____

A. Movie previews have often helped producers decide what parts of movies they should leave in or take out. For example, the first preview of King Kong in 1933 was very helpful. In one scene, four men were first attacked by Kong and then eaten by giant spiders. Many members of the audience ran screaming from the theater and would not return. The premiere of the 1950 film Sunset Boulevard was also very helpful. In the original opening scene, William Holden was in a morgue with thirty-six other "corpses," discussing the ways some of them had died. When he began to tell them of his life with Gloria Swanson, the audience found this hilarious. They were supposed to take the scene seriously. The result was a delay of six months in the release of the film while a new beginning was added.

B. Movie previews have often helped producers decide whether they should change various parts of a movie. After the 1933 preview of King Kong, a scene in which four men who had been attacked by Kong were eaten by giant spiders was taken out as many people ran screaming from the theater and would not return. The 1950 premiere of Sunset Boulevard also led to some changes. In the original opening scene, William Holden was in a morgue talking with thirty-six other "corpses" about the ways some of them had died. When he began to tell them of his life with Gloria Swanson, the audience found this hilarious, instead of taking the scene seriously.

C. What do Sunset Boulevard and King Kong have in common? Both show the value of using movie previews to test audience reaction. The first 1933 preview of King Kong showed that a scene showing four men being eaten by giant spiders after having been attacked by Kong was too frightening for many people. They ran screaming from the theater and couldn't be coaxed back. The 1950 premiere of Sunset Boulevard was also a scream, but not the kind the producers intended. The movie opens with William Holden lying in a morgue discussing the ways they had died with thirty-six other "corpses." When he began to tell them of his life with Gloria Swanson, the audience couldn't take him seriously. Their laughter caused a six-month delay while the beginning was rewritten.

D. Producers very often use movie previews to decide if changes are needed. The premiere of Sunset Boulevard in 1950 led to a new beginning and a six-month delay in film release. At the beginning, William Holden and thirty-six other "corpses" discuss the ways some of them died. Rather than taking this seriously, the audience thought it was hilarious when he began to tell them of his life with Gloria Swanson. The first 1933 preview of King Kong was very helpful for its producers because one scene so terrified the audience that many of them ran screaming from the theater and would not return. In this particular scene, four men who had first been attacked by Kong were eaten by giant spiders.

4.
I. It is common for supervisors to view employees as "things" to be manipulated.   4.____
II. This approach does not motivate employees, nor does the carrot-and-stick approach because employees often recognize these behaviors and resent them.
III. Supervisors can change these behaviors by using self-inquiry and persistence.
IV. The best managers genuinely respect those they work with, are supportive and helpful, and are interested in working as a team with those they supervise.
V. They disagree with the Golden Rule that says "he or she who has the gold makes the rules."

A. Some managers act as if they think the Golden Rule means "he or she who has the gold makes the rules." They show disrespect to employees by seeing them as "things" to be manipulated. Obviously, this approach does not motivate employees any more than the carrot-and-stick approach motivates them. The employees are smart enough to spot these behaviors and resent them. On the other hand, the managers genuinely respect those they work with, are supportive and helpful, and are interested in working as a team. Self-inquiry and persistence can change even the former type of supervisor into the latter.
B. Many supervisors all into the trap of viewing employees as "things" to be manipulated, or try to motivate them by using a carrot-and-stick approach. These methods do not motivate employees, who often recognize the behaviors and resent them. Supervisors can change these behaviors, however, by using self-inquiry and persistence. The best managers are supportive and helpful, and have genuine respect for those with whom they work. They are interested in working as a team with those they supervise. To them, the Golden Rule is not "he or she who has the gold makes the rules."
C. Some supervisors see employees as "things" to be used or manipulated using a carrot-and-stick technique. These methods don't work. Employees often see through them and resent them. A supervisor who

wants to change may do so. The techniques of self-inquiry and persistence can be used to turn him or her into the type of supervisor who doesn't think the Golden Rule is "he or she who has the gold makes the rules." They may become like the best managers who treat those with whom they work with respect and give them help and support. These are the manager who know how to build a team.

D. Unfortunately, many supervisors act as if their employees are objects whose movements they can position at will. This mistaken belief has the same result as another popular motivational technique—the carrot-and-stick approach. Both attitudes can lead to the same result—resentment from those employees who recognize the behaviors for what they are. Supervisors who recognize these behaviors can change through the use of persistence and the use of self-inquiry. It's important to remember that the best managers respect their employees. They readily give necessary help and support and are interested in working as a team with those they supervise. To these managers, the Golden Rule is not "he or she who has the gold makes the rules."

5.
I. The first half of the nineteenth century produced a group of pessimistic poets—Byron, De Musset, Heine, Pushkin, and Leopardi.
II. It also produced a group of pessimistic composers—Schubert, Chopin, Schumann, and even the later Beethoven.
III. Above all, in philosophy, there was the profoundly pessimistic philosopher, Schopenhauer.
IV. The Revolution was dead, the Bourbons were restored, the feudal barons were reclaiming their land, and progress everywhere was being suppressed, as the great age was over.
V. "I thank God," said Goethe, "that I am not young in so thoroughly finished a world."

5.____

A. "I thank God," said Goethe, "that I am not young in so thoroughly finished a world." The Revolution was dead, the Bourbons were restored, the feudal barons were reclaiming their land, and progress everywhere was being suppressed. The first half of the nineteenth century produced a group of pessimistic poets: Byron, De Musset, Heine, Pushkin, and Leopardi. It also produced pessimistic composers: Schubert, Chopin, Schumann. Although Beethoven came later, he fits into this group, too. Finally and above all, it also produced a profoundly pessimistic philosopher, Schopenhauer. The great age was over.
B. The first half of the nineteenth century produced a group of pessimistic poets: Byron, De Musset, Heine, Pushkin, and Leopardi. It produced a group of pessimistic composers: Schubert, Chopin, Schumann, and even the later Beethoven. Above all, it produced a profoundly pessimistic philosopher, Schopenhauer. For each of these men, the great age was over. The Revolution was dead, and the Bourbons were restored. The feudal barons were reclaiming their land, and progress everywhere was being suppressed.

C. The great age was over. The Revolution was dead—the Bourbons were restored, and the feudal barons were reclaiming their land. Progress everywhere was being suppressed. Out of this climate came a profound pessimism. Poets, like Byron, De Musset, Heine, Pushkin, and Leopardi; composers, like Schubert, Chopin, Schumann, and even the later Beethoven; and above all, a profoundly pessimistic philosopher, Schopenauer. This pessimism which arose in the first half of the nineteenth century is illustrated by these words of Goethe, "I thank God that I am not young in so thoroughly finished a world."

D. The first half of the nineteenth century produced a group of pessimistic poets, Byron, De Musset, Heine, Pushkin, and Leopardi—and a group of pessimistic composers, Schubert, Chopin, Schumann, and the later Beethoven. Above it all, it produced a profoundly pessimistic philosopher, Schopenhauer. The great age was over. The Revolution was dead, the Bourbons were restored, the feudal barons were reclaiming their land, and progress everywhere was being suppressed. "I thank God," said Goethe, "that I am not young in so thoroughly finished a world."

6. I. A new manager sometimes may feel insecure about his or her competence in the new position.
   II. The new manager may then exhibit defensive or arrogant behavior towards those one supervises, or the new manager may direct overly flattering behavior toward one's new supervisor.

   A. Sometimes, a new manager may feel insecure about his or her ability to perform well in this new position. The insecurity may lead him or her to treat others differently. He or she may display arrogant or defensive behavior towards those he or she supervises, or be overly flattering to his or her new supervisor.
   B. A new manager may sometimes feel insecure about his or her ability to perform well in the new position. He or she may then become arrogant, defensive, or overly flattering towards those he or she works with.
   C. There are times when a new manager may be insecure about how well he or she can perform in the new job. The new manager may also behave defensive or act in an arrogant way towards those he or she supervises, or overly flatter his or her boss.
   D. Sometimes a new manager may feel insecure about his or her ability to perform well in the new position. He or she may then display arrogant or defensive behavior towards those they supervise, or become overly flattering towards their supervisors.

6.____

7. I. It is possible to eliminate unwanted behavior by bringing it under stimulus control—tying the behavior to a cue, and then never, or rarely, giving the cue.
   II. One trainer successfully used this method to keep an energetic young porpoise from coming out of her tank whenever she felt like it, which was potentially dangerous.
   III. Her trainer taught her to do it for a reward, in response to a hand signal, and then rarely gave the signal.

7.____

A. Unwanted behavior can be eliminated by tying the behavior to a cue, and then never, or rarely, giving the cue. This is called stimulus control. One trainer was able to use this method to keep an energetic young porpoise from coming out of her tank by teaching her to come out for a reward in response to a hand signal, and then rarely giving the signal.
B. Stimulus control can be used to eliminate unwanted behavior. In this method, behavior is tied to a cue, and then the cue is rarely, if ever, given. One trainer was able to successfully use stimulus control to keep an energetic young porpoise from coming out of her tank whenever she felt like it—a potentially dangerous practice. She taught the porpoise to come out for a reward when she gave a hand signal, and then rarely gave the signal.
C. It is possible to eliminate behavior that is undesirable by bringing it under stimulus control by tying behavior to a signal, and then rarely giving the signal. One trainer successfully used this method to keep an energetic porpoise from coming out of her tank, a potentially dangerous situation. Her trainer taught the porpoise to do it for a reward, in response to a hand signal, and then would rarely give the signal.
D. By using stimulus control, it is possible to eliminate unwanted behavior by tying the behavior to a cue, and then rarely or never give the cue. One trainer was able to use this method to successfully stop a young porpoise from coming out of her tank whenever she felt like it. To curb this potentially dangerous practice, the porpoise was taught by the trainer to come out of the tank for a reward, in response to a hand signal, and then rarely given the signal.

8.
I. There is a great deal of concern over the safety of commercial trucks, caused by their greatly increased role in serious accidents since federal deregulation in 1981.
II. Recently, 60 percent of trucks in New York and Connecticut and 70 percent of trucks in Maryland randomly stopped by state troopers failed safety inspections.
III. Sixteen states in the United States require no training at all for truck drivers.

8.____

A. Since federal deregulation in 1981, there has been a great deal of concern over the safety of commercial trucks, and their greatly increased role in serious accidents. Recently, 60 percent of trucks in New York and Connecticut, and 70 percent of trucks in Maryland failed safety inspections. Sixteen states in the United States require no training at all for truck drivers.
B. There is a great deal of concern over the safety of commercial trucks since federal deregulation in 1981. Their role in serious accidents has greatly increased. Recently, 60 percent of trucks randomly stopped in Connecticut and New York and 70 percent in Maryland failed safety inspections conducted by state troopers. Sixteen states in the United States provide no training at all for truck drivers.
C. Commercial trucks have a greatly increased role in serious accidents since federal deregulation in 1981. This has led to a great deal of concern.

Recently, 70 percent of trucks in Maryland and 60 percent of trucks in New York and Connecticut failed inspection of those that were randomly stopped by state troopers. Sixteen states in the United States require no training for all truck drivers.

D. Since federal deregulation in 1981, the role that commercial trucks have played in serious accidents has greatly increased, and this has led to a great deal of concern. Recently, 60 percent of trucks in New York and Connecticut, and 70 percent of trucks in Maryland randomly stopped by state troopers failed safety inspections. Sixteen states in the U.S. don't require any training for truck drivers.

9.
I. No matter how much some people have, they still feel unsatisfied and want more, or want to keep what they have forever.
II. One recent television documentary showed several people flying from New York to Paris for a one-day shopping spree to buy platinum earrings, because they were bored.
III. In Brazil, some people were ordering coffins that cost a minimum of $45,000 and are equipping them with deluxe stereos, televisions, and other graveyard necessities.

9._____

A. Some people, despite having a great deal, still feel unsatisfied and want more, or think they can keep what they have forever. One recent documentary on television showed several people enroute from Paris to New York for a one day shopping spree to buy platinum earrings, because they were bored. Some people in Brazil are even ordering coffins equipped with such graveyard necessities as deluxe stereos and televisions. The price of the coffins start at $45,000.
B. No matter how much some people have, they may feel unsatisfied. This leads them to want more, or to want to keep what they have forever. Recently, a television documentary depicting several people flying from New York to Paris for a one day shopping spree to buy platinum earrings. They were bored. Some people in Brazil are ordering coffins that cost at least $45,000 and come equipped with deluxe televisions, stereos and other necessary graveyard items.
C. Some people will be dissatisfied no matter how much they have. They may want more, or they may want to keep what they have forever. One recent television documentary showed several people, motivated by boredom, jetting from New York to Paris for a one-day shopping spree to buy platinum earrings. In Brazil, some people are ordering coffins equipped with deluxe stereos, televisions and other graveyard necessities. The minimum price for these coffins—$45,000.
D. Some people are never satisfied. No matter how much they have they still want more, or think they can keep what they have forever. One television documentary recently showed several people flying from New York to Paris for the day to buy platinum earrings because they were bored. In Brazil, some people are ordering coffins that cost $45,000 and are equipped with deluxe stereos, televisions and other graveyard necessities.

10. I. A television signal or video signal has three parts.
    II. Its parts are the black-and-white portion, the color portion, and the synchronizing (sync) pulses, which keep the picture stable.
    III. Each video source, whether it's a camera or a video-cassette recorder contains its own generator of these synchronizing pulses to accompany the picture that it's sending in order to keep it steady and straight.
    IV. In order to produce a clean recording, a video-cassette recorder must "lock-up" to the sync pulses that are part of the video it is trying to record, and this effort may be very noticeable if the device does not have gunlock.

10.____

   A. There are three parts to a television or video signal: the black-and-white part, the color part, and the synchronizing (sync) pulses, which keep the picture stable. Whether it's a video-cassette recorder or a camera, each video source contains its own pulse that synchronizes and generates the picture it's sending in order to keep it straight and steady. A video-cassette recorder must "lock up" to the sync pulses that are part of the video it's trying to record. If the device doesn't have gunlock, this effort must be very noticeable.
   B. A video signal or television is comprised of three parts: the black-and-white portion, the color portion, and the sync (synchronizing) pulses, which keep the picture stable. Whether it's a camera or a video-cassette recorder, each video source contains its own generator of these synchronizing pulses. These accompany the picture that it's sending in order to keep it straight and steady. A video-cassette recorder must "lock up" to the sync pulses that are part of the video it is trying to record in order to produce a clean recording. This effort may be very noticeable if the device does not have gunlock.
   C. There are three parts to a television or video signal: the color portion, the black-and-white portion, and the sync (synchronizing pulses). These keep the picture stable. Each video source, whether it's a video-cassette recorder or a camera, generates these synchronizing pulses accompanying the picture it's sending in order to keep it straight and steady. If a clean recording is to be produced, a video-cassette recorder must store the sync pulses that are part of the video it is trying to record. This effort may not be noticeable if the device does not have gunlock.
   D. A television signal or video signal has three parts: the black-and-white portion, the color portion, and the synchronizing (sync) pulses. It's the sync pulses which keep the picture stable, which accompany it and keep it steady and straight. Whether it's a camera or a video-cassette recorder, each video source contains its own generator of these synchronizing pulses. To produce a clean recording, a video-cassette recorder must "lock up" to the sync pulses that are part of the video it is trying to record. If the device does not have gunlock, this effort may be very noticeable.

KEY (CORRECT ANSWERS)

1.	C	6.	A
2.	B	7.	B
3.	A	8.	D
4.	B	9.	C
5.	D	10.	D

FINDING A JOB

TABLE OF CONTENTS

	Page
INTRODUCTION	1
PLANNING YOUR TIME	2
DETERMINING YOUR JOB SKILLS	3
MATCHING YOUR BACKGROUND AND EXPERIENCE TO JOBS	4
WHERE TO GET JOB INFORMATION	4
COVER LETTERS AND APPLICATIONS	6
PREPARING YOUR RESUME	6
10 TIPS FOR THE EFFECTIVE RESUME	8
COMMON QUESTIONS ABOUT RESUMES	9
INTERVIEWING	10
COMMON QUESTIONS ABOUT INTERVIEWS	11
TESTING	13
AFTER THE INTERVIEW	14
JOB SEARCH CHECKLIST	15
MOST COMMON JOB-HUNTING MISTAKES	16
COMMON QUESTIONS ABOUT THE FOLLOW-UP	18
AFTER YOU ARE HIRED	18

FINDING A JOB

INTRODUCTION

You need a job. Somewhere, an employer has the job you want. How do you get that job? By marketing your job talents. By showing employers you have the skills they need.

Do you have job talents? Yes! Homemakers, disabled individuals, veterans, students just out of school, people already working—all have skills and experience for many good jobs.

What you need to know is how to market your talents effectively to find the right job. This guide will help you to:

- Evaluate your interests and skills
- Find job information
- Write resumes and application letters
- Prepare and plan for job interviews
- Plan your time
- Take tests

PLANNING YOUR TIME

Now is the best time to start looking for a job. You're as qualified as other applicants, so start now before someone else gets "your" job. You've already made a good start by reading this guide!

What's the most important thing to know about your job search?
<u>Finding work is a full-time job.</u>

In a full-time job, you:
* Have responsibilities (work duties and procedures)
* "Punch a clock" or be at work "on time"
* Work hard all day, 40 hours a week
* Report to a boss, who makes sure you carry out your responsibilities

To find a job, you must:
* Set your own responsibilities (things you must do every day to get a job)
* Wake up early at a set time to start looking for work
* Look hard for a job, all day, 40 hours a week
* Be your own boss (or appoint a friend to be your "boss") to make sure you carry out your job search responsibilities

Tips for Planning an Effective Job Search:

- Make a "To Do List" every day. Outline daily activities to look for a job.
- Apply for jobs early in the day. This will make a good impression and give you time to complete applications, have interviews, take tests, etc.
- Call employers to find out the best times to apply. Some companies take applications only on certain days and times during the week.
- Write down all employers you contact, the date of your contacts, people you talk to, and special notes about your contacts.
- Apply at several companies in the same area when possible. This saves time and money.
- Be prepared. Have a "master application" and resumes, pens, maps and job information with you all the time. Who knows when a "hot lead" will come your way.
- Follow up leads immediately. If you find out about a job late in the day, call right then! Don't wait until the next day.
- Network. Tell everyone you know that you're looking for a job. Stay in touch with friends and contacts. Follow up new leads immediately.
- Read pamphlets and books on how to get a job. The time you spend reading these materials will save you a lot of time in your job search.
- Make automated connections through systems on the Internet, such as America's Job Bank and the Talent Bank.

DETERMINING YOUR JOB SKILLS

Another tip for finding the right job: *Make a list of your background experience.*

If you think you don't have any experience—think again! You may not have specific job experience, but you do have work experience. You have "worked" as a homemaker, a student, a volunteer, in a hobby or some other personal activity. The skills you use for these "jobs" can be applied to other jobs.

A background and experience list may help you to fill out job applications, provide information for job interviews and prepare resumes (if you're applying for professional or office jobs).

Tips for Making a Background and Experience List:

Interests and Aptitudes
- List your hobbies, clubs you belong to, sports you're involved in, church and school activities, and things that interest you. List things you are good at or have special ability for.
- Look at the first item on your list. Think about the skills or talents it takes to do that item. Really think about it! All hobbies, activities, etc. take a lot of skills, knowledge and abilities. For example, playing basketball requires the ability to interact with others (be a "team player") and the ability to lead or direct teammates/coworkers. Homemaking requires the ability to manage budgets, handle multiple tasks and the skills to teach or train others. Fixing cars requires knowledge of electronics and machinery, and the ability to diagnose mechanical problems.

Work History
If you've worked before, list your jobs. Include volunteer, part-time, summer and self-employment. Next, write down work duties for the jobs you listed. Now think about the skills and talents it took to do each work duty. Write them down.

Education
- List the schools you attended, dates, major studies or courses completed. Include military and vocational education and on-the-job training
- List degrees, certificates, awards and honors
- Ask yourself what classes or training you like and why

Physical Condition
- Do you have any disabilities limiting the kind of work you can do? Companies will often make special accommodations to employ disabled persons (in fact, some accommodations are legally required). If you have strong or special physical capabilities, list these too.

Career Goals
- What kind of work do you want to be doing 5 or 10 years from now? What kind of job could you get now to help you reach this goal?

MATCHING YOUR BACKGROUND AND EXPERIENCE TO JOBS

Look at the abilities (talents) identified on your background and experience list. You have talents that you use every day. Now find out what jobs can use your talents.

Start at your local State Employment Service Office ("Job Service"). This office has free information about many jobs. You may be given an appointment with a career counselor who can help you decide what kind of work is best suited to your abilities and interests.

While you're at Job Service, ask to see the *Guide for Occupational Exploration* and the *Occupational Outlook Handbook* (you can also get these books at most public libraries). These easy-to-read books, published by the Department of Labor, describe work duties for different occupations, skills and abilities needed for different types of jobs, how to enter occupations, where jobs are located, training and qualifications needed, as well as earnings, working conditions and future opportunities.

Match the skills and abilities in your list to the skills and abilities of different jobs. Don't limit yourself. The important thing is not the job title, but the skills and abilities of the job. You may find that your abilities match with an occupation that you have never thought about.

WHERE TO GET JOB INFORMATION

If you know what job skills you have, you are ready to look for a job. You can look for job openings at these sources:

- Networking – Tell everyone you know you're looking for a job. Ask about openings where your friends work.
- Private employers – Contact employers directly to market your job talents. Talk to the person who would supervise you even if there are no jobs currently open.
- State Employment Service Offices provide help on finding jobs and other services, such as career counseling
- America's Job Bank – A nationwide pool of job opportunities which will extend your search to other states and can be viewed in your local Employment Service offices or on the Internet at http://www.ajb.dni.us
- Federal, state and local government personnel offices list a wide range of job opportunities. Check the government listings in your phone book.
- Local public libraries have books on occupations and often post local job announcements. Many state libraries are also providing free access to Internet through PCs.
- Newspaper ads list various job openings
- Local phone book – Look for career counseling centers in your area
- Private employment and temporary agencies offer placement (employer or job hunter may pay a fee)
- Community colleges and trade schools usually offer counseling and job information to students and the general public
- Proprietary schools – Private training centers offer instruction in specific trades (tuition is usually required). Check with your office of state education for credible schools.

- Community organizations such as clubs, associations, women and minority centers, and youth organizations
- Churches frequently operate employment services or provide job search help
- Veterans' placement centers operate through State Employment Service Offices. Veterans' social and help organizations often have job listings for members.
- Union and apprenticeship programs provide job opportunities and information. Contact your state apprenticeship council or relevant labor union directly.
- Government sponsored training programs offer direct placement or short-term training and placement for applicants who qualify. Check the yellow pages under Job Training Programs or Government Services.
- Journals and newsletters for professional or trade associations often advertise job openings in their field. Ask for these at the local library.

Under the Civil Rights Act of 1964, as amended in 1991, all of the sources listed above serve persons of any race, color, religion, sex or national origin. The Age Discrimination in Employment Act of 1967 forbids agencies to discriminate against older workers. Both laws forbid employers to discriminate in hiring.

In addition, the Americans with Disabilities Act under Title I prohibits employment discrimination against "qualified individuals with disabilities." A qualified individual with a disability is: an individual with a disability who meets the skill, experience, education and other job-related requirements of a position held or desired, and who, with or without reasonable accommodation, can perform the essential functions of a job.

MOST COMMONLY USED JOB SEARCH METHODS

Percent of Jobseekers Using this Method	Method	Effectiveness Rate
66.0%	Applied directly to employer	47.7%
50.8	Asked friends about jobs where they work	22.1
41.8	Asked friends about jobs elsewhere	11.9
28.4	Asked relatives about jobs where they work	19.3
27.3	Asked relatives about jobs elsewhere	7.4
45.9	Answered local newspaper ads	23.9
21.0	Private employment agency	24.2
12.5	School placement office	21.4
15.3	Civil Service test	12.5
10.4	Asked teacher or professor	12.1
1.6	Placed ad in local newspaper	12.9
6.0	Union hiring hall	22.2

COVER LETTERS AND APPLICATIONS

A letter of application is used when inquiring about a job or submitting an application form. If you're applying for a job that requires a resume, you should write a cover letter to accompany your resume. The purpose of these cover letters is to:
- Tell how your job talents will benefit the company
- Show why the employer should read your resume or application form
- Ask for a job interview

Tips for Writing Cover Letters
- Write a separate letter for each job application
- Type letters on quality 8 1/2" x 11" paper
- Use proper sentence structure and correct spelling and punctuation
- Convey personal interest and enthusiasm
- Keep your letter short and to the point
- Show that you've done some homework on the company (you know what they do, their interests and problems)
- Try to identify something about you that is unique or of interest to the employer
- Request an interview, and if possible, suggest a date and time
- Include your address and telephone number
- Address each letter to the specific person you want to talk to (the person who would actually supervise you)
- Highlight your job qualifications
- State the position you are seeking and the source of the job opening

PREPARING YOUR RESUME

You want to apply for a job. Do you need a resume? That depends on the kind of job you are applying for:

* Professional, technical, administrative and managerial jobs, as well as sales, secretarial, clerical and other office jobs require a resume.

* Skilled jobs (ex. baker, hotel clerk, electrician, drafter, welder, etc.) sometimes require a resume.

* Unskilled, quick turnover jobs (ex. fast food server, laborers, machine loader, etc.) do not require a resume.

Tips for Good Resumes

You need two types of information to prepare your resume:
1. Self-information – You need to know your job talents, work history, education and career goals. Did you complete your background and experience list? If you did, you have the self-information required to prepare your resume.
1. Job information – Gather specific information on the job you're applying for. Here's what you need:
    - Job duties (to match your skills to the skills needed for the job). Get your job duties from the job announcement. If the announcement or ad is vague, call the employer and ask for a description of job duties.
    - Education and experience required
    - Hours and shifts usually worked

- Pay range (make their top offer the minimum acceptable!)

With the information on yourself and the job you're applying for, you're ready to write your resume.

Two Types of Resumes

Reverse Chronological -- lists jobs you've had. Your most recent job is listed first, your job before that is listed second, and so on. Each job has employment dates and job duties.

Functional -- describes your skills, abilities and accomplishments that relate to the job you're applying for. Employment history is less detailed than chronological resumes.

What kind of resume should you use? Answer the following questions:
- Have you progressed up a clearly defined career ladder, and you're looking for job advancement?
- Do you have recent job experience at one or more companies?

If you're answer is yes, use a reverse chronological resume.

- Are you a displaced homemaker?
- Are you a veteran and you want to relate your military training to civilian jobs?
- Do you have little or no job experience?
- Do you have gaps in your work history?
- Is the job you're applying for different from your present or recent job?
- Do you want to emphasize your work skills and accomplishments instead of describing your job duties?

If your answer to any of these is yes, use a functional resume.

Tips for Preparing a Functional Resume
- Study the duties for the job you're applying for. Identify two or three general skills that are important to the job.
- Review your background and experience list. Find talents and accomplishments that demonstrate your ability to perform the job skills.
- List your talents and accomplishments under the job skills they relate to
- Use simple, short, active sentences
- Focus attention on strong points

Tips for Preparing a Reverse Chronological Resume
- List your jobs starting with your present or most recent job. Give exact dates for each job.
- Briefly describe the main duties you performed in each job
- Emphasize duties that are important for the job you're applying for
- Use simple, short, active sentences
- Include scholarships and honors and major school subjects if related to your job goal

10 TIPS FOR THE EFFECTIVE RESUME

The following rules apply to all resumes:

1. If possible, use a computer to prepare your resume. There are computer programs that make it easy to produce a professional looking resume. Your local school, library, Employment Service local office or "quick print" shop can help.
1. Do not include irrelevant personal information (age, weight, height, marital status, etc.)
1. Do not include salary and wages
1. Center or justify all headings – Don't use abbreviations
1. Be positive and identify accomplishments
1. Use action verbs
1. Be specific – Use concise sentences, keep it short (one page is best)
1. Make sure your resume "looks good" (neat and readable)
1. Proofread the master copy carefully. Have someone else proofread it also.
1. Inspect photocopies for clarity, smudges and marks

Action Verbs

Action verbs give your resume power and direction. Try to begin all skills statements with an action verb. Here is a sample of action verbs for different types of skills:

Management	Technical	Clerical	Communication
administered	assembled	arranged	arranged
analyzed	built	catalogued	addressed
coordinated	calculated	compiled	authored
developed	designed	generated	drafted
directed	operated	organized	formulated
evaluated	overhauled	processed	
improved	remodeled	persuaded	
supervised	repaired	systemized	

Creative	Financial	Helping	Research
conceptualized	administered	assessed	clarified
created	analyzed	coached	evaluated
designed	balanced	counseled	identified
established	budgeted	diagnosed	inspected
fashioned	forecast	facilitated	organized
illustrated	marketed	represented	summarized
invented	planned		
performed	projected		

The Talent Bank

Once a resume is completed, it can be fed into the Talent Bank, now available in many local Job Service offices. The Bank is an electronically searchable database of resumes or other statements of qualification from job hunters seeking employment. Those searching for jobs or new opportunities can post their resumes/qualifications to the bank. Employers search the banks to select a group of resumes for further screening.

COMMON QUESTIONS ABOUT RESUMES

What is the purpose of a resume?
To obtain an interview. This can be quite a challenge since the average resume receives only 5-7 seconds of viewing. No one is ever hired solely on the basis of how they look on paper. The resume is your promotional literature for selling yourself. It serves to whet an employer's appetite and make him or her want to know more about you.

How do I accomplish that purpose?
By providing the most relevant information in as concise a manner as possible: the most positive, impressive highlights from your past that would be applicable to the position you seek.

What's a good way to start?
Describing yourself on paper is difficult and somewhat dehumanizing. Make a list of information about yourself, set it aside and add to it later. Place the accumulated data in a format that best emphasizes your strengths and delete the least relevant information.

What's important to emphasize?
Focus on what you have achieved and learned and not just on how and where you have spent your time. Be as specific as possible in citing examples to support your statements. Emphasize only your very best side, the information most applicable to the job at hand. Use only the most impressive tip of the iceberg that also relates to the employer's needs. Editing is difficult, but be sure not to bury the most relevant and attractive information in too much irrelevant detail.

I feel like I'm bragging.
There's no room for modesty in a job search. Employers expect to see ideal candidates, and those who don't portray themselves as such are seldom given the benefit of the doubt. Don't lie, but don't sell yourself short. Save being humble for the interview.

Is tone important in a resume?
Tone is the personality that comes through on a resume—sentence structure, word usage, etc. It can say as much about you as the content.

What is a "statement of objective?"
This is a sentence or two at the beginning of your resume that tells a prospective employer at a glance if you are a possible match for their needs. It is both general, so as to not exclude you from openings you might be interested in, yet specific, so it does communicate some boundaries to the employer. It is essential for individuals with extensive unrelated experience.

What if all my experience is unrelated to my objective?
You might want to summarize the various skills you have learned in past jobs, and emphasize the skills you've acquired that would be relevant in the prospective position. You should consider a functional resume.

What should not be included in a resume?
Information unrelated to your job objective. Also avoid using a picture, height and weight, Social Security number, and other personal information, as well as

misspelled and incorrectly used words, slang or jargon, abbreviations, and flowery or overused adjectives and phrases.

How creative should I be?

Try to be somewhat creative, but you want your resume to stand out through its content. Being overly creative with the appearance or format of the resume may turn off some employers.

What else should I know?

Standard length is one page. Avoid using "I" since this is assumed; use action verbs to describe duties and accomplishments. Use different resumes for different job types. Heavier paper gives the resume a more professional look, and be sure it is free of smudges or stray marks. Be sincere, appropriate, and keep the information relevant.

Where do I distribute the resume?

Have the resume prepared to send to all individuals you contact. You can also attach it to applications, and be sure to send a cover letter along with the resume, introducing yourself and describing your experiences to the employer. All your information should be sent to the person you have been in contact with who has the authority to hire you. Be sure to confirm spellings of names and accuracy of titles.

INTERVIEWING

Most hiring decisions are made at the first interview. How you come across in that interview could be as important as your experience and job talents. Here are some interviewing tips that will help you get the job you want:

Before the Interview
- Learn as much as you can about the company salary and benefits. Friends, neighbors and relatives who work for the company are good sources of information. Libraries, local chambers of commerce, etc. are also helpful.
- Learn everything you can about the job and how your previous experience and training qualify you for the job.
- Write down the things you will need to complete applications (background and experience list, resume or work summary, samples of work if applicable, etc.)
- Be sure to bring your social security card, driver's license, union card, military records, etc.

The Interview
- Dress for the interview as you would for the job. Don't overdress or look too informal.
- Always go to the interview alone. Arrange for babysitters, transportation and other pitfalls ahead of time so that you can be on time and relaxed in the interview.
- Find common ground with the employer. Pictures, books, plants, etc. in the employer's office can be conversation topics.
- Express your interest in the job and the company using information you gathered to prepare for the interview
- Let the interviewer direct the conversation

- Answer questions in a clear and positive manner. Show how your experience and training will make you productive in the shortest time with minimal supervision.
- Speak positively of former employers and coworkers no matter why you left even if you were fired from your last job
- Let the employer lead into conversation about benefits. Your focus on these items can be a turn off. But, don't be afraid to ask questions about things you really need to know.
- When discussing salary, be flexible—avoid naming a specific salary. If you're too high, you risk not getting the job. If you're too low, you undersell yourself. Answer questions on salary requirements with responses such as, "I'm interested in the job as a career opportunity so I'm negotiable on the starting salary." Negotiate, but don't sell yourself short.

Closing the Interview
- If the employer does not offer you a job or say when you will hear about it, ask when you may call to find out about the decision
- If the employer asks you to call or return for another interview, make a written note of the time, date and place
- Thank the employer for the interview and reaffirm your interest and qualifications for the job

COMMON QUESTIONS ABOUT INTERVIEWING

What is the objective of an interview?
For the employer, it is to see if your paper image and portrayal stand up in real life: to see if you are a match for the position at hand. Your objective should be to explore whether or not this is a place you'd like to work. Formulate open-ended questions and probe. Look for indicators.

Do I have to dress up?
Yes, although more formal dress is usually most appropriate, gear yourself to the dress standards of the particular workplace. When in doubt, dress up to show you take the interview seriously.

How do I make an impression?
Be yourself. Smile. Use a firm handshake and make frequent eye contact. Elaborate on information from your resume that indicates you will work out well, that there is little risk in hiring you, and that you have a steady, predictable record of dedication. Be confident.

What should I bring?
Extra copies of your resume, and any other items that may be appropriate and relevant to the job. Be sure to provide these items at the proper point of the interview.

What is the best way to prepare?
List all the questions you think will be asked, talk to someone in the field or in a similar position, role-play with a friend or roommate, or any other activity that you feel will help you prepare.

How do I get information about the position or interviewer, or both?
Many firms are willing to send you a job description if you ask for one. It is possible to get a wealth of information about companies and even individuals on the Internet, or even from a library. College placement offices also have brochures, reports and other related information.

How do I get information during an interview?
You will always be given a chance to ask questions. Remember, though, that good interviewers will control the interview so that they first get all the information they want about you before they tell you too much about the job. In this way they avoid "telegraphing"—revealing the "right" answers to their questions.

How can I get them talking first?
After you answer a question, ask one. This will make the interview more conversational and natural. Ask open-ended questions like "In what direction is the company moving?" or "How would a typical day on the job be spent?"

What other techniques might the interviewer use?
If the interviewer has been trained well, he or she might "funnel" questions from general to specific—meaning they may begin by asking about general experience with customer service, followed by asking of any particular instances or bad experiences and how you handled them specifically.

How honest should I be?
Be honest, but not blunt. Don't offer negative information that is unnecessary or irrelevant. At the same time, you'll fit in best if you leave no surprises, especially about your abilities.

What if I'm asked a question I can't answer?
You more than likely will not be quizzed during your interview. A question that throws you can be handled by asking for clarification or an example, and if you still do not know, say so. However, too many "I don't knows" may indicate you failed to do enough preparation.

Will I be asked any trick questions?
Maybe. They will probably be concerned with how serious you are about this career, profession and particular job. They may ask about other alternatives or positions you may be considering, to which you want to appear as though you are focusing on this job exclusively. A common response by you may be, "Since this is exactly what I'm looking for, I've postponed looking at other positions. If I'm not accepted, I would probably check with (competitor)." Be aware that some employers have in mind certain answers or responses to certain questions that may disqualify you, so be careful how you field questions regarding future plans, other jobs, etc.

What should I ask about?
Whatever is necessary to meet your criteria for selection, and to give you a good feel for the job, the people and the working environment. Some topics to ask about are responsibilities, time commitments, co-workers, travel, style of management, the selection process, etc. Find out what your first day, week and month would be like on the job, and be able to explain how you would approach these responsibilities.

What questions will likely be asked?
The following is a list of common questions taken from interview evaluation forms and used frequently by many employers:

Why should I hire you?
What are your current job expectations?
Describe your educational background.
What was your favorite course in school? Why?
Describe the previous jobs you have had, beginning with your most recent.
What were your major responsibilities in your last job?
What are some of the things you did particularly well in your last job? Or achieved the greatest success in?
Why did you leave your last job?
What were some of the negative qualities of your last job?
What did you like most/least about your past jobs and academic work?
Describe something you did that was not normally part of your job.
Do you like working with figures?
What do you think are the qualities of a good supervisor?
What do you consider to be the perfect job for you?
What do you feel have been your most significant accomplishments?
Give an accurate description of yourself.
Would you have any trouble making it to work by 8:00 a.m.?
Describe what you see as your major strengths and weaknesses for the position.
Are there certain things you feel more confident about doing? What are they, and why do you feel the way you do?
If you had a choice of responsibilities within this department, which would you prefer?
How do you perceive your role in interacting with other department members?
What key factors attract you to this position or company?
What do you see yourself doing in five years?
How much independence and flexibility do you like in a job?
What do you expect for a starting salary?
When can you start?

TESTING

For some jobs, you may need to take a test. Usually, the job announcement or ad will say if a test is required. There are several types of selection and job fitness tests:

- Aptitude tests predict how easily you will learn the job and how well you perform job tasks
- Job knowledge and proficiency tests measure what you know and what you can do in a job (for example, word processing speed for a secretary job, knowledge of street names and routes for a firefighter job, etc.)
- Literacy tests measure reading and arithmetic levels
- Personality tests help identify your personal style in dealing with tasks and other people. Certain personalities can be well suited for some jobs and not so well suited for other jobs. For example, an outgoing person may be well suited for a sales job.
- Honesty and Integrity tests evaluate the likelihood of stealing and trustworthiness of applicants
- Physical ability tests measure strength, flexibility, stamina and speed for jobs that require physical performance
- Medical examinations and tests determine physical fitness to do a job
- Drug tests show the presence of illegal drugs that could impair job performance and threaten the safety of others

How to Prepare for Tests

You can't study directly for aptitude tests. But you can get ready to do your best by learning as much as you can about the test by taking other tests. Look for tests or quizzes in magazines and school books. Set time limits. By taking tests, you learn about the testing process. This will help you feel more comfortable when you are tested.

Brush up on your skills. For example, if you are taking a typing test, practice typing. If you're taking a construction test, review books and blueprints. Get ready for physical tests by doing activities similar to those required for the job. For literacy tests, review and do exercises in reading and math books or enroll in remedial classes.

It's natural to be nervous about tests (some anxiety may even help you). Here are some tips that will help you take most tests:

1. Make a list of what you need for the test (pencil, eyeglasses, ID, etc.) Check it before leaving.
2. Get a good night's sleep
3. If you're sick, call and reschedule the test
4. Leave for the test site early
5. If you have any physical difficulties, tell the test administrator
6. If you don't understand the test instructions, ask for help before the test begins
7. If there are strict time limits, budget the time. Don't linger on difficult questions.
8. Find out if guessing is penalized. If not, guess on questions you're not sure about.
9. If you have time, review your answers. Check to make sure you did not misread a question or make careless mistakes.
10. You may be able to re-take the test. Ask about the re-testing policy.
11. Get a proper interpretation of your scores. The scores may indicate other career opportunities that should be pursued.

AFTER THE INTERVIEW

Make each interview a learning experience. After it's over, ask yourself these questions:

- What points did I make that seemed to interest the employer?
- Did I present my qualifications well? Did I overlook qualifications that were important for the job?
- Did I learn all I needed to know about the job?
- Did I ask questions I had about the job?
- Did I talk too much? Too little?
- Was I too tense? Too relaxed?
- Was I too aggressive? Not aggressive enough?
- Was I dressed appropriately?
- Did I effectively close the interview?

Make a list of specific ways you can improve your next interview. Remember, "practice makes perfect" – the more you interview the better you will get at it.

If you plan carefully and stay motivated, you can "market your job talents." You will get a job that uses your skills and pays you well.

JOB SEARCH CHECKLIST

Complete items 1-3 on the checklist before starting your job search
Complete items 4-5 every day of your search
Complete items 6-9 when you have interviews

1. Identify Occupations
   - Make a background and experience list
   - Review information on jobs
   - Identify jobs that use your talents

2. Identify Employers
   - Ask friends, relatives, etc. to help you look for job openings
   - Go to your State Employment Service Office for assistance
   - Contact employers to get company and job information
   - Utilize other sources to get job leads
   - Obtain job announcements and descriptions

3. Prepare Materials
   - Write resumes – use job announcements to match your skills with job requirements
   - Write cover letters or applications
   - Assemble a job search kit (pens, maps, guides, background list, etc.)
   - Use the Talent Bank

4. Plan Your Time
   - Wake up early to start looking for work
   - Make a "to do" list of everything you'll do to look for a job
   - Work hard all day to find a job
   - Reward yourself

5. Contact Employers
   - Call employers directly (even if they're not advertising openings)
   - Talk to the person who would supervise you if you were hired
   - Go to companies to fill out applications
   - Contact friends and relatives to see if they know about openings
   - Use America's Job Bank on the Internet

6. Prepare for Interviews
   - Learn about the company you're interviewing with
   - Review job announcements to determine how your skills will help you do the job
   - Assemble resumes, forms, etc.

7. Go to Interviews
   - Dress right for the interview – go alone
   - Be clean, concise, positive
   - Thank the interviewer

8. Evaluate Interviews
   - Send a hand-written thank you note to the interviewer within 24 hours
   - Think about how you could improve the interview

9. Take Tests
   - Find out about the test(s) you will be taking
   - Brush up on job skills
   - Relax and be confident

10. Accept the Job!
    - Understand job duties and expectations, work hours, salary, benefits, etc.
    - Be flexible when discussing salary (but don't sell yourself short)
    - Congratulations!

THE MOST COMMON JOB-HUNTING MISTAKES

1. Not taking action – Putting off decisions, phone calls, leads, writing, looking. Not doing anything constructive. Avoiding even thinking about doing something. Making excuses, limiting yourself, erecting roadblocks to progress, complaining and generally procrastinating.

2. Not reflecting enough – Not thinking about what is wanted, ideal or possible. Jumping to the search and jumping too often to the wrong job, simply because it appeared first.

3. Not taking advantage of all potential resources – Overlooking the assistance and leads that can be found in talking with friends, parents, professors, etc. Not using libraries or the Internet. Hesitating to call people you don't know.

4. Not exploiting skills and experience – Not understanding the unique value, strengths and marketability of your past.

5. Not being committed to the job search – Not making adequate time for preparing and searching, or not giving it the highest priority.

6. Not empathizing with the employer's perspective – The employer has needs, time frames, problems and constraints that may or may not be compatible with yours.

7. Not being positive – Underestimating the power of attitude on the process and the employer.

8. Not anticipating and practicing for an interview – Not being able to relate your abilities to the employer's needs. Not role-playing and formulating a strategy for success.

9. Not following up in a professional manner – Thank-you letters, even after rejection, can make a name for you in what may prove to be a small, closely knit profession.

Below, in rank order, are reasons business and industrial managers gave for not offering a job to a new graduate, based upon a survey by Frank S. Endicott, former Director of Placement of Northwestern University:

1. Poor personal appearance
2. Overbearing know-it-all
3. Inability to express self clearly; poor voice, diction, grammar
4. Lack of planning for career; no purpose or goals
5. Lack of confidence and poise
6. Lack of interest and enthusiasm
7. Failure to participate in activities
8. Overemphasis on money; interest only in best dollar offer
9. Poor scholastic record—just got by
10. Unwilling to start at the bottom—expects too much too soon
11. Makes excuses, evasiveness, hedges on unfavorable factors in records
12. Lack of tact
13. Lack of maturity
14. Lack of courtesy
15. Condemnation of past employers
16. Lack of social understandings
17. Marked dislike for school work
18. Lack of vitality
19. Fails to look interviewer in the eye
20. Limp, fishy handshake
21. Indecision
22. Loafs during vacations preferring lakeside pleasures
23. Unhappy married life
24. Friction with parents
25. Sloppy application blank
26. Merely shopping around
27. Only wants a job for short time
28. Little sense of humor
29. Lack of knowledge of field of specialization
30. Parents make decision for them
31. No interest in company or industry
32. Emphasis on who they know
33. Unwillingness to go where we sent them
34. Cynical
35. Low moral standards
36. Lazy
37. Intolerant with strong prejudices
38. Narrow interests
39. Spends much time in movies
40. Poor handling of personal finances
41. No interest in community activities
42. Inability to take criticism
43. Lack of appreciation of value of experience
44. Radical ideas
45. Late to interview without good reason
46. Never heard of company
47. Failure to express appreciation for interviewer's time
48. Asks no questions about the job
49. High-pressure type
50. Indefinite response to questions

COMMON QUESTIONS ABOUT THE FOLLOW-UP

How important is the thank-you letter?
Thank-you letters have been found to be the only correlation between people who are looking for positions and those who get hired. They've been found to correlate even more than qualifications, amount of experience or degree of interest.

What is involved in a good thank-you letter?
This is usually personal, explaining your interest in the position, referring to a topic which was discussed, or providing more indicators of how well you'll fit in. More information about your qualifications, an example of your work and alternative solutions to a problem which you learned of during the interview would all be appropriate. This letter serves to concisely remind them of you at the time of the employment decision.

When should I send it?
You should send a hand-written letter within 24 hours of the interview.

Is timing important?
Yes. Most job processes, including selections and applicant review, are RANDOM. The most qualified applicant is often buried beneath those who were a bit more aggressive and marketed themselves more effectively. Hence, the more leads you pursue, the greater chance of success.

How can I be persistent without being overbearing?
Proper follow-up is more a matter of the right timing, not the quantity of contacts. Ask when the decision is being made, or check back when you feel they've reviewed your resume or are making the hiring decision after your interview.

What should I do if I think I'm being stalled?
Employers often put an applicant on hold. This may be because they are waiting for final approval of the position or because they think they can attract more qualified applicants if they delay. You can force the issue subtly by alluding to another job offer, or you can be more blatant by giving a date by which you need to know. Either method indicates you have a sense of value and self-worth and are not willing to be put off. Be careful not to appear too demanding though.

I was rejected, but I have no idea why.
Chances are small that you'll ever be given the real reason. If you felt you had a good chance, you should persist and acquire information that can help you for your next interview.

AFTER YOU ARE HIRED

- Come to closure with hanging leads – Contact any employers who are still considering you and tell them you've found a job, and thank them for their interest. Regardless of the profession you choose, you can be certain it is a tight network. You may want to work for one of those employers later, or keep in contact with them in your current position.
- Learn to listen
- Learn the background of your area – The history of the people and the development of departmental responsibilities can help give you indicators of

- the written and unwritten "rules" of the field, and what changes can be expected.
- Learn the informal power network – Bear in mind that power is often outside the formal structure. Who is respected and who is not? Whose opinion of you is going to matter more than anything you do?
- Make time for people as well as the task – Focus on doing a good job, but also be sure to concentrate on developing good relationships with those you work with. Both are important. Be sensitive to your place within the hierarchy.
- Be sensitive to processes – What may seem slow or inefficient might serve a valuable purpose that is not initially apparent. Learn through observing.
- Keep the right attitude and perspective – Be appreciative of the opportunity long after you are hired. No matter what may be asked of you, try to treat each assignment as a learning experience.
- Use your resources to their fullest potential – Take advantage of all the options available to you to learn in your current environment. Taking part in projects and committees can be beneficial and show you are interested. Learn all you can as soon as you can.

www.ingramcontent.com/pod-product-compliance
Lightning Source LLC
Chambersburg PA
CBHW081812300426
44116CB00014B/2328